SHATTERED, and Then …

A Journey to Sexual Healing and Integration

By Laurie Morris

Shattered, and Then …
A Journey to Sexual Healing and Integration
by Laurie Morris

Printed in the United States of America

ISBN 978-1-60477-622-5

www.xulonpress.com

DEDICATION PAGE

To David Morris, my precious husband and the man I loved with all my heart. He was a man who passionately loved God. He pursued holiness with tenacity, honesty and vulnerability. Bravely uncovering his sin before men so that he could be healed and represent His Lord in purity. I'm eternally thankful to him for releasing me to tell our story before he left this earth. My deep gratitude also goes to my children, and to David's family, for releasing me to include portions of their stories.

SPECIAL THANKS:

A special thanks to Jill Mitchell for challenging me to write this book. I could not have finished the book without her input and Eleanor Perry-Smith, Gloria Cotten, JoAnna McKethan and Connie Reagan's insight and editing skills. You all are awesome!

ENDORSEMENT PAGE:

"These words were not cheaply written. Laurie's life has been shaped in the sometimes agonizing crucible of personal experience. But she doesn't stay there. Laurie radiates life and forgiveness as she relates her story. The message is clear. No matter where you have been or what you have been through there is healing. This is a book of hope."

Senior Pastor Michael Fletcher, author
Manna Church
Fayetteville, NC

"Laurie Morris has a burning passion to see the children of God set free from every hindrance of soul that keeps them from fulfilling the destiny God has prepared for them. This motivation makes her book more than a personal testimony of redemption, more than a courageous exposé of the deceptive hand of the enemy, though it is both of these. This book is, in fact, powerful, intimate, effective, one-on-one ministry between Laurie and the reader. Her life-stories impart hope, her clear, uncluttered teaching from the scripture engenders faith for healing. The power of the Holy Spirit is in this book!"

Gloria Cotton, author
Antioch Ministries, NC

"Gutsy! That's the word that I use to describe Laurie Morris and "Shattered, and Then..." She has addressed hot topics that are still considered taboo by some, and yet daily language by others. Thank you Laurie for speaking vital truth in love with a holy boldness that is absolutely critical in this hour. Consume reading this love story, written from a place of victory, leaving each one of us with a challenge and a responsibility."

Jill Mitchell, President
Kingdom Connections International, Inc.
Houston, Texas

TABLE OF CONTENTS

INTRODUCTION

It was 1980. I was attending Christ for the Nations Institute, in Dallas. Our guest speaker that week was David Wilkerson. He was preaching on how Satan comes to "steal the precious seed" of destiny, through childhood sexual abuse and hidden sexual sin, from those who have a call to serve God, especially when there's a ministry call in the arenas of worship and prayer. As I listened, I felt like the room became a vortex of frozen time. His words were alive and somehow I KNEW that he was prophesying truth about my future. I wept through the entire message in intercession as the words were written on my soul. Little did I know then, but the word God wrote on my heart that day would become a part of my call as a wife and as a leader in the body of Christ.

My walk into the world of sexual abuse and its ramifications began intensely when I married my husband the following year. He had been sexually abused from the age of three by a man in relationship with his family. His parents had no idea. Because of the abuse, he struggled with homosexuality the bulk of his adult life. Our journey to wholeness was very long. There was always a potential for shame from the church at large. We told our story countless times as we privately ministered to many broken people in the body of Christ – several of them leaders as we were. Many precious friends and leaders walked with us in prayer and healing to see us both come to wholeness.

For some time now, I have had a passion burning in my heart to tell of the freedom we achieved through honesty and submission to one another and to God. I want to impart hope to those on the fringes of the church as well as church leaders who are struggling to walk in holiness and are, more than likely, alone. Our story is one that is usually hidden in shame and covered over with silence by the church. How could a man of God struggle with this sin? How could he lead people in worship? Were our lives in Christ even valid while struggling with this? What was wrong with me and why did I stay in the marriage?

Recently the church has been reminded that not just the "average Joe" in the church is struggling to walk clean. Leaders too, sometimes struggle with addictive sin. Is their failure to confess their weakness just the result of pride? Could it be that their hesitancy to confess is due, at least in part, to the fact that history has proven that the church will react with a sword instead of help?

All too frequently, the church has failed to examine the fruit of people's lives and relationships when promotion was at hand. Promotion is too often given to an engaging, charismatic personality, who has obvious gifts, without enough regard for under-lying character and the evidence of the fruit of the Spirit. This premise has contributed to some leaders in the Body of Christ being in key positions of authority, while not being prepared to battle against attacks on their own moral purity. The spirit of the age has been one of sexual deviance of every kind, and it invades even the church.

Today I hear the voice of God calling with His mercy and with His Spirit of TRUTH to come out of her "ostrich in the sand" position into a stance that confronts the forces of wickedness and brokenness in the power of Almighty God. I believe God is equip-ping His Church to minister healing to herself. This silence that I am breaking now is the call of God not only for today, but also for future generations who are called to holiness and victory.

I have been privileged to minister to countless leaders and just regular sheep for the past twenty-plus years in the area of sexual brokenness. The numbers of hurting individuals is growing, not shrinking. The statistics are staggering in reference to those who have been touched by sexual brokenness. National estimates from the Community Coalition to Prevent Family Violence, project that one in three girls is sexually abused before the age of eighteen and one in six boys. This is for sexual abuse alone. However, it is estimated that almost 75% of legitimate cases go unreported at all. I use an inclusive term of broken-ness above, because I am referring to anyone touched by sexual betrayal of any kind, i.e. rape, voyeurism, infidelity, etc. I pray as you read this testimony of victory and instruction you will be encouraged, and that your eyes may be opened and that the Lord may use this instrument to uncover deeds of darkness, bringing restoration.

CHAPTER 1

The Man of My Dreams

It was January 18, 1981 and I was a wreck. It was raining outside and humid as a sauna. I had just come from a time of intercession in the prayer room at the Bible school I was attending in Dallas, Texas. I was looking a bit ragged, my hair falling out of a bun, and I was late for one of my flute students. I rushed into the music department and ran into someone coming around the corner. WOW! It was a guy with unbelievably vivid blue eyes boring into mine. Looking into those baby blues I felt my spirit/soul do a somersault. I knew this was the man of my dreams, literally. The man I would marry. This was "The One" the Lord had told me about six months previously during a time of fasting. I introduced myself and asked his name. "David Morris," he replied. This was the guy I was supposed to meet with to see if he could accompany me on the piano! I asked him if we could set up a practice for the song I was going to do in a few months. He responded by saying we should just try it out now. I agreed and we proceeded to a practice room and began a run through of the song. About an hour later, a friend heard us practicing and invited us to minister in music the following Friday night at a coffee house. I was nervous and excited that we would be connecting again so soon, and the night at the coffee house went great. We just seemed to "fit" when we were singing together. I had "stars in my eyes" already.

We spent the next three weeks "falling madly in love." As we talked we found that we even had the same vision for our lives! Each of us believed that God had called us to lead His people in worship to new places of power and intimacy. David was my kind of guy – funny and great looking. He also dressed nice and was smart! He was musical and liked to communicate! WOW — all the KUDOS! Best of all, he passionately loved God and was a man of the Word. He proposed to me just three weeks later. How bizarre! Yet it seemed everyone thought it was a match made in heaven – God's couple!

But underneath the external excitement was a serious rumbling of warning in my spirit. I felt there were some places of brokenness in David that I needed to look at before saying yes to marriage. I moved frequently in the word of knowledge mentioned in I Corinthians 12:8 after receiving the Baptism of the Holy Spirit at age seventeen. I had also been raised around my mom ministering to people who were hurting. I knew something was deeply wounded in David. No external cues clued me in, rather, an internal sensing.

Reality Check

By a word of knowledge I perceived that David struggled with sexual issues...specifically that he had been sexually abused. I also heard the faintest whisper from God about homosexuality. I approached David tentatively about these things one afternoon a few weeks into dating. I told him I was sensing a deep area of wounding sexually in his life that he needed to tell me about. Immediately, he began to share his deep pain and shame over the fact that he had been sexually abused as a toddler. He never had been able to fully identify the person who abused him, but it was a male. He then shared about his concurrent struggle with homosexuality. I wept tears of brokenness with David that the enemy had come in to destroy him at such an early age. I was so touched by his willingness to trust me with this vulnerable place.

But then I heard the Lord say quietly and firmly, "Laurie, he will be unfaithful to you - do you still want to marry him?" I, in my "need to be a savior mode," said yes. I rationalized that the infidelity the Holy Spirit had warned me of would be a one time occurrence, and not that bad. I thought God had made me a strong woman and that I was up for the challenge.

Little did I know the difficulty of the journey that we were about to begin! Every belief system I had would be challenged and crushed by the difficult path that lay ahead. Many times we interpret what God has spoken to us through our filter of need or expectation. There are many of us walking around mad at God for His leading and our following what we *thought* we heard Him say. God didn't say to me, "He'll be unfaithful to you one time – do you want him?" But *I* put that little spin on His words in my mind.

We don't realize how our own mechanisms set us up for complications in life. Have you ever met anyone who is a Christian yet has had bad relationships one right after another? Perhaps you know someone who has been repeatedly abused emotionally or physically? I've asked individuals like these about their relationships with God. On the surface, they may appear to be emotionally healthy, but as one delves deeper it's evident that a piece of their identity is broken or distorted. (I will talk about our broken identity piece in a later chapter.) Not until many years later did I realize, through counseling, that my own broken identity piece and my savior complex played a role in David and my hooking up.

Even with God's hand on our lives, we often forget how our mindsets can lead us into difficult circumstances. Psychologists tell us that people are drawn to other people by their past patterns. For instance, a battered woman is often drawn to another abuser, or a sexual abuse victim is drawn to marry someone with sexual issues. These are typical examples of what psychologists call patterning. With sexual abuse the pattern can be referred to as sexual imprinting. We are drawn to act out what was experienced as a child over and over in some manner. We create expectations from our experiences that lead to certain behaviors from others and ourselves.

Another term used to describe this pattern spiritually is a soul tie. Soul ties keep us bound to another human being, not because of a healthy motivation but because of something in our souls that is broken. Picture it like the tentacles of an octopus reaching out into the invisible realm. Because of sexual involvement, not forgiving, or strong emotional involvement, there are invisible, yet strong ties in the spirit that keep us tethered to another person. It is so important if you are not married yet, to make sure all doorways of your past are closed and healed. If broken places remain in your soul, they can draw you into a relationship that may not be God's best. If you are married, then dealing with past wounds can free you from inappropriately reacting to and manipulating your mate.

Seen from the outside, David's and my story appeared to be one of tremendous favor and blessing. Our lives were indeed blessed and our gifts obviously given by God. David had begun playing the piano by ear at the age of three, and writing songs by the age of five. I had been trained to play the piano and flute. We both also sang. David had a particularly awesome voice. However, we were both extremely broken vessels emotionally. At Christ for the Nations, the bible school we attended at the time, we were the "golden couple." The anointing fell on us when we ministered in music and the Lord would come and touch His people.

We began a glorious season of getting to know one another and being used together by the Father. However, the fractures in our pots were starting to weaken under the pressure of ministering and being exalted by men. I had all kinds of religious perspectives and David had his own issues, from his extremely controlling, religious upbringing.

We knew from the moment we met that we didn't want to pursue the typical road in music of performance and recording, but that we were called and set apart to be worshippers and Psalmists, creators of music the Lord could "pray" through. David had even been prophesied over in-utero, that he was called as a Psalmist by God. Even though our bible school taught deliverance, we didn't have a clue about how to stand against the plan the enemy had set up to destroy us — particularly David. With our fragile pots under pressure, the enemy was going to succeed shortly in ensnaring him.

David and I both had been taught about generational blessings and curses as quoted in Exodus 20:5, "For I the Lord your God am a jealous God visiting the iniquity of the fathers on the children on the third and fourth generations." We knew we had some warfare ahead of us regarding our families. My grandfather had been a 33rd level Mason. He had opened up all kinds of occult doors to his family by the vows and curses he had invoked towards us. I use the term occult because of the blood covenants that are made at the higher levels. (For those of you not familiar with Freemasonry, I suggest some reading materials in the Resources section of the book.) David's family had struggled for generations with sexual issues and addictions before they were saved.

David had, on numerous occasions, gone for prayer for deliverance from his "demons." The results were very negative emotionally for him, because he still felt controlled by his impulses at times and this fact caused him to believe he had somehow failed in his approach to the Father. The overall mindset in the 80's was one of "just get delivered," and if you weren't "delivered," then you were not repentant. So we blindly proceeded in seeking God together for freedom and believing in desperation that He would heal us in and through worship alone.

True — God is able to heal us instantly from some of our wounds through worship, because "we shall be like Him because we shall see Him just as He is." I John 3:2. But it is not God's pattern to instantly deliver people without recognition of what damaged them in the first place! His goal is for us to be able to minister out of the journeys we have taken. He wants us to have a glimpse of what He truly accomplished for us personally on the cross. God wants applied knowledge of healing! He wants an experiential receiving of His grace, not just a positional one. Even with all the counseling emphasis in the public now - Oprah, Dr. Phil, and Gary Marshall - there are still many individuals in the Body of Christ who don't believe that their history affects how they function in the present. Believing it or not believing it, doesn't change the fact that we are driven by our experiences and mindsets from our past.

The human soul can wonderfully compartmentalize issues. Some personality types succeed at this better than others. David and I were both great at it! We took some of our past emotional events and buried them for years. This is a coping mechanism called disassociation. The recognition of the impact of these events sometimes doesn't hit us until we are provoked by another crisis. Just because we have buried our feelings doesn't mean they are not affecting us! Basically this was my situation. I lived for years in denial about my true feelings and about what was occurring in our relationship. Added to this, I had never processed my own issues concerning the loss of my father. It took a crisis in the form of depression to shake me and make me look at what was really going on in my soul.

CHAPTER 2

Facing Codependency – It's All About Me

At the time David and I met, I was still bound by a terrible wound in my soul concerning how I saw myself. I related to men on a deep need level because of the loss of my dad. I was at the very vulnerable age of twelve, when he died suddenly at only 38 years of age. To make matters worse, I was way ahead of my age in physical development. Not only was I an early bird, but also an oversized one! I was extremely large on top (think Dolly Parton) and created a stir wherever I went because of gawking men and boys. By the time I was in high school I was the token football mascot and the brunt of jokes for all the guys, both Christian and non-Christian alike! I was approached numerous times by photographers wanting me to pose for Playboy or be in wet t-shirt contests. However embarrassing this was, I felt no insult, just a weird affirmation. Concurrently, I was driven by the need for someone to replace my dad in my life so I made a high priority of finding "the one" man for me. I truly had no clue of my deep hurts and the emotions I buried for years, stemming from these events.

In the year before I met David, my mom convinced me to have breast reduction surgery. I was in pain daily, doctors told me my spine was curving, and I felt I couldn't go on in the public eye with my appearance being so distracting. I was referred to as the "twin towers" by some of the athletic community at Oral Robert's University, where I attended school for one year. I also was feeling a call to full-time ministry. Can you imagine me leading people in worship and resembling a Playboy bunny? Not good! So at my mom's loving insistence, I decided to go ahead with the surgery.

I was not prepared for the change in the way men looked at me and approached me. Somehow, distorted or not, I had felt that I was beautiful and attractive because of all the male attention I received. Though most of it was lustful and perverted, it still made me feel beautiful. I was not prepared for the sudden lack of attention, albeit bad attention. The surgery did not go as well as I had hoped and left me with severe scarring. I was devastated and convinced no one would want me now that I was "marred."

Part of my unconsciously held belief system surfaced: I thought I was unlovable unless I looked and behaved perfectly. I believed that no one would love me if they really knew what was underneath the surface. This was only one distorted piece of my identity puzzle. Another "biggy" was my daddy wound.

His sudden death with no good-byes had created a huge void of abandonment in my life. I had a loving relationship with him and with God the Father, but huge fears and issues of responsibility crept into my thinking patterns after his death. I felt responsible in some way. My mom didn't know how to cope with her widowhood and pain, and quickly remarried. In light of our new life we locked up our grief as a family. Add this to an already very performance-oriented, religious mindset and I was "co-dependent waiting to happen."

Into this unhealthy picture came David. I responded with all my first-born, savior mentality: "Here's someone to love me!" "Someone needs me." "I can help save him," were just some of my uncon-scious, distorted motivations. Thus I began a journey of idolatry with my husband. I didn't recognize it as such, but I focused all my energy into seeing him attain healing and freedom. My goal was to get him to accept and love me because I did everything right.

I wasn't aware of it, but I was also looking for Father God's approval of me. These unspoken goals were not His biblical pattern for marriage. Yikes! But the unspoken goals existed none the less! I was incredibly lost on the journey to knowing God. Here I was, a Spirit-filled believer, taught in the Word and supposedly helping lead His people towards Him, when I didn't really know Him myself! Now this is a very scary picture outside of the mercy of a forgiving God who knew I wanted to walk in righteousness before Him. Thank God He uses broken vessels every moment of every day to pour His truth through!

I put every effort into being "on guard" to pray for David, to watch and listen. I wanted to be the perfect wife, intercessor and partner. Part of a woman's call as a helpmeet is to be an intercessor – one who prays, and has her ear to the ground. We are to war in prayer on our husband's behalf. The word helpmeet means to come alongside, but in my initial broken approach I was codependent and controlling. My unconscious motives were an attempt, again, at being his savior! I'm sure that self-protection from the infidelity that God had warned me about was functioning as well. God knew I truly wanted to help David, but no one can do that job but Jesus. I was moving in idolatry by making David my focal point and not the Father. How self-righteous it was to think that I could save him from a life of homosexuality! Consequently, we developed a very dependent relationship and it wasn't until years down the road, that I was able to see it.

David, on the other hand, was desperately looking for acceptance and someone to love him in spite of his struggles. His own struggle with Obsessive Compulsive Disorder (OCD) caused him to play the role of the controller in our relationship. To an outsider, I would appear to be the dominant one in our relationship, as he did not like confrontation and I was more verbally assertive. At home though, I tended to be the "doormat" in the relationship.

David was constantly raising the standard of what he needed and expected of me. "Honey, the closet would look so much neater if you just hung everything the same way." "Honey, just let me show you a better way to wash those dishes" etc. I yielded to his "suggestions" with enthusiasm for many years because of my fear of rejection and failure. We both had made a verbal promise to always be the first one to admit being wrong when arguing, but I was the only one following through with that commitment! I had it down to a science. Sounds a bit like a clip from the movie "The Stepford Wives!" I was functioning under perverted submission and I was obeying David's wishes above the Lord's.

Our marriage was a perfect picture of co-dependency, a widely used term in the Body of Christ today. Because of its familiarity, so often we apply the term co-dependence to lives but forget that there is a remedy for this condition in Christ. Co-dependence may be the diagnosis but the condition does not have to be permanent! We need to move past the diagnosis, into breaking its cycle, and digging up its root causes. Restoration from co-dependency comes when we receive healing from the soul injuries that produce the need in us to control. We do this by receiving healing from hurts that cause us to control. David and I eventually, got there!

Let me define co-dependency a bit. One person becomes totally enmeshed with another, to the exclusion of everyone else. As the relationship develops, this person invests all of his hope and trust completely in this human relationship instead of in God. A co-dependent belief system says that I cannot achieve my destiny without that other person. What a deception this is! Each of us stands before God alone, not with anyone else! Not even our spouse can support us when we stand before God. The Bible teaches us that we are all individual parts of one Body, and that we are to support one another. We are to dwell in unity. However, it is not appropriate to focus all of our attention on just one part of the body!

Being vulnerable and accountable to another person is important for every Christian, but accountability can become idolatrous if we put our faith and trust in a person above God. If we seek one person or group's approval above the Father's, or treat them as if we couldn't live without them, then we are falling into co-dependency and idolatry. It took several events of crisis in our lives for me to begin to recognize my ungodly patterns of co-dependency. God will use whatever He can to draw us to Himself!

The first major crisis came when David betrayed his marriage vows. At the time, we were on staff at a church in Dallas. Through this experience, God attempted once again to shake me out of my denial systems, but I retreated to the la-la land of Christianity that says: "Just forgive, and peace will come." "The perfect Christian wife doesn't get angry but forgives." I believed erroneously, that I couldn't let David see my hurt because that wouldn't be true forgiveness. I was very good at living in this place of denial! I was so good at it, that when we were sent to see a Christian counselor for the first time, I invalidated a personality test because of these denial mechanisms! I tried so hard to give the "right" answers, that I was unable to be truthful about my feelings. Imagine the shock, after spending about three hours taking a test that was to help aid in our healing, being told that I had managed to negate the test!

I was functioning with very unhealthy emotional behaviors! I was not allowing pain, and anger and grief to surface in me. The Bible never negates emotion or forbids expressing it. It talks about the lives of many godly people in their pain, sorrow, and anger. The Psalms are full of David's honest confrontation of his emotions before God. Psalm 142:2-3 says, "I pour out my complaint before Him and I declare my trouble before Him, when my spirit was overwhelmed within me." Psalm 42:5 says, "Why are you in despair oh my soul?" It says in Psalm 55:4-5, "My heart is in anguish within me and the terrors of death have fallen upon me. Fear and trembling come upon me and horror has overwhelmed me." The Bible comforts us with the statement that God holds our tears in His bottle. (Psalm 56:8) And Jesus Himself bore our sorrows not just our sin. (Isaiah 53:4)

One of the ways I had tried to protect David was by not letting him see the devastation and pain that his infidelity had wrought. I knew he had not wanted to hurt me intentionally, so I rationalized that it would be godlier not to expose him to my raw emotions. It was scary for both of us to learn to reveal our heart's condition to one another. But as I chose to become healthy and show David what I was feeling and release him to God, he in turn did the same with me. We began to trust GOD for David's deliverance.

Please don't suppress or deny your deep emotions! Suppression leads to angst and depression. Don't proclaim you are FINE when that isn't true! Let me tell you what FINE really means. Feeling Intensely Negative Emotions! It's a great Christian cover-up for hiding feelings of anger and hurt. Look at Psalm 6:1-4. It reads: ".... Be gracious to me oh Lord, for I am pining away. Heal me oh Lord for my bones are dismayed, and my soul is greatly dismayed. But you oh Lord, how long? Return oh Lord and rescue my soul." Do you think that David was possibly hurt and confused here? Was he sad and desperate? Fighting through hopelessness? Many Christians believe that anger is not acceptable to God, but His Word says to be angry and not sin. (Ephesians 4:26) Pour out your complaints to God. Let Him help you work through your hurt. Don't just live with depression or say you are fine! Confront what is underneath your hopelessness and fear.

Because of my co-dependant mindset in our early years, I was also constrained by yet another lie. I believed that my destiny had been circumvented because of the consequences of David's struggles. I believed that I was somehow trapped and not fully able to be all that I was created to be.

One day the Lord spoke to me, "You hold the keys to your own cage." I didn't really understand what He meant. I kept asking for more information from Him. Eventually a friend, who moved prophetically, came to me and shared a vision she'd had. She saw a gilded bird cage with a bird inside on the swing bar. The door to the cage was OPEN and there was a key on the floor of the cage. The bird was a picture of me crying out that I was trapped. Revelation flooded my soul as I realized the Lord was explaining what

He'd said to me. NO MAN held the reins to my life. I had the keys to my own cage. God was the one who was in charge of my destiny. It was so liberating to no longer blame David for the restraints that I had attributed to him. I began to believe I could be all I was destined to be. It was liberating for him as well. When I quit holding him responsible, he became free from my limiting accusations!

One of the more revelatory moments in my life was related to my denial mechanisms. I knew the Lord said in scripture that "our heart is deceitfully wicked and we don't know it." I acknowledged this in prayer for years, by asking God to uncover hidden sins in me. However, when we pray that kind of prayer and God answers, it doesn't always look the way we thought it would. I sincerely wanted to uncover deception in myself. But when the Lord finally did it, I was shocked!

Remember when I talked about the mechanisms that draw us together just from the soul realm alone? We create expectations from our past experiences that create unhealthy behaviors in ourselves and draw inappropriate behaviors out of others. Well, parts of my soul were talking very loudly and I was unaware of what was driving them.

Let me explain. David said to me for YEARS that I would make a certain face at him that was angry and demeaning. I would tell him that there was nothing in my heart like that towards him and he must be misperceiving me. We went around that mountain hundreds of times over the years. I, of course, said he had an issue with his mom and he, of course, said he didn't! One day in the midst of scolding one of our kids, I suddenly became aware of this evil thing — and it was emanating from me! I stopped, utterly taken aback. I knew instantly that I was demeaning my child and that I had done it countless times to David. I had never before been aware of it. I couldn't believe it! I immediately called him crying and truly repented to him. I was finally awakened to my horribly, broken response mechanism! David was very happy and loved being validated! That's a guy for you!! I was totally flabbergasted at my soul's deception concerning the condition of my heart. By now you would think I would have a clue about my soul's varied mechanisms and not be shocked!

Remember, God is always looking for truth in US – not just the other person. God is concerned with our relationship with Him first and our spouse second. It doesn't matter what they have done to us. *Our* response is what matters to Him. I want to encourage you again. Repent and deal with any dependency issues in your relationships, so as not to keep that person, or yourself, from their destiny. Face any locked up emotions you have suppressed about any situation in your past. Let God have His full work in you and that person! Let Him focus on you and bring His revelation to you about your hidden issues. You will experience tremendous freedom and hope into your life!

Father, I ask the Holy Spirit to come and bring revelation to my sister/brother of any areas of idolatry or buried pain in their relationships. Uncover it and as they repent, bring Your healing and grace to change their mindsets. Increase their ability to trust You with every aspect of their lives. Come and let your spotlight highlight them, and reveal any hidden places of deception or denial. In Jesus' Name.

CHAPTER 3

Betrayal

Betrayal is most often associated with broken marriage vows or relationships that have been severed by a singular event, but I want to cover some of the other forms of betrayal as well. The ramifications of broken trust that ripple out from the event of betrayal often do as much damage as the event itself. Sometimes, the precise act of betrayal is not what destroys one's soul, and overwhelms lives and emotions, but the consequences or circumstances that are created by that betrayal.

In my eighth month of pregnancy, with our first child Brooke, David came to me and confessed some past moral failures, most pre-marital. At that time, I was only able to process my emotions on the surface. So I did what my fragile soul could handle at the time. I went into total suppression of my shock and pain. (The land of denial I talked about earlier.) I promptly forgave David and felt nothing except for some brief sorrow.

Perhaps you can imagine the amount of unre-
leased emotion communicated to Brooke in-utero. I
was unable to even begin to look at my anger and
pain. This resulted in Brooke receiving my stress
in her unborn state. After her birth, it was evident
in her behavior that she had been damaged by my
suppressed trauma. She was an adorable, but very
serious baby. She didn't smile or laugh very often.
She also didn't seem to want to bond with her dad.
She would scream and cry if he was home with her
alone. We didn't immediately recognize her behavior
as being related to the emotional damage done to her
little soul. Eventually we realized this and began
asking the Lord to heal her. He led us to pray over
her at various stages, asking the Holy Spirit to bring
healing to the areas of her heart damaged in the
womb.

As Brooke grew, we used appropriate honesty
in these prayer times and saw visible changes in her
demeanor and responses. The following is a paraphrase of some things we prayed with her when she
was still quite small. I began with a brief explanation
of, "Mommy was really upset with your dad when
you were in my tummy. I didn't want to be, but he'd
hurt me. Even mommies and daddies who love each
other hurt each other sometimes. Will you forgive me
Brooke for sharing lots of negative feelings with you
when you were in my tummy? Can Mommy just pray
for a minute over you for the Holy Spirit to come and
heal your heart there?" Then we prayed, and the few
times we did this kind of healing prayer, the Lord met
her with wisdom and grace. There was an immediate

change in her interactions with her dad after this and they became very close in the years to come.

For any of you who are thinking at this point – "whoa, she's nuts!" Please reference some of these other sources that support the effects a woman's emotional state can have on her unborn children. John and Paula Sanford's book titled "Healing the Wounded Spirit" and "An Integrated, Biblical Approach to Healing," by Chester and Betsy Kylstra are both very descriptive in their explanation of this phenomenon. I expect there are some of you reading this that have struggled with issues during your lifetime that can be traced back to the time your mom was pregnant with you.

I am thinking particularly of anyone who is adopted or has an adopted child. Often there are issues of abandonment and rejection that plague individuals from this situation. These emotional roots go back to the birth mother's feelings during pregnancy. Praying with someone you trust, who is led by the Holy Spirit, can bring tremendous breakthrough in previously blocked areas of your heart. I have witnessed countless women and men who were stuck in a particular area of their life. After going round and round the mountain with the same cycle of pain, they would ask the Lord to reveal the root of their hurts. Many times the Holy Spirit has led them back to the time when they were in their mother's womb. As they allowed the Holy Spirit to speak to them, they discovered they had heard or felt something in-utero, that had a profound effect on them. After praying over the event, these individuals received breakthrough. Change in their behaviors and responses to life occurred because healing had occurred at the root source. As I shared earlier, I can personally attest to this fact with my daughter.

Betrayal came knocking again, when our first and only son, Collin, was born. By this time we were full-time ministers at our local church in Dallas. We were experiencing an apex of joy, as David had done an Integrity Hosanna Recording and the son he had longed for was born. Then BAM – another confession of inappropriate behavior with someone we knew well. I was freaking out as I warred with all the questions and emotions erupting inside. Was I going to lose this other family's friendship? What about the relationships between our children? Were we going to have to publicly confess details of the indiscretion?

Unfortunately, the answer was "yes" to our losing our friendship as it had existed. I was deeply saddened and angry about this. When the one we love betrays us with someone we know all kinds of repercussions occur. We ended up having to totally change the way we related to this couple. There were some activities we had shared as families that we could no longer participate in. We had to come up with an explanation for our children as to why we no longer hung out together. Our future plans had to be dropped as well.

Most of us don't really recognize how loss or betrayal will impact the dynamics of our relationships, even the casual relationships. Other people don't know how to respond to us, so they don't.

They are afraid of saying the wrong thing, so they're silent. Avoidance is the number one way of coping for most people, even if they aren't directly involved. The result is that the initial betrayal is compounded by the seeming rejection of many other people. We experienced this personally from the casual relationships around us. Those who were acquaintances would look away or turn away if they saw us coming. I am convinced that this was because they didn't know what to say. Over all, we were incredibly blessed that most of our intimate friends did not abandon us or isolate from us. But a few didn't know how to cope with David's confession and promptly withdrew their friendship from us. Sadly this is very common.

We experienced several types of losses resulting from our broken marriage vows, and there was so much grief. Something had died. Life was never going to be the same. Fear came in with our pain. We had to face, as many couples do where there has been infidelity, the real possibility of having contracted a disease. I was a terrified wreck when we both had to get tested for AIDS other infectious diseases. We were incredibly fortunate that David had neither contracted nor passed along anything. Many couples are not so fortunate. A few ladies, with whom I walked with to wholeness, did contract a disease from their spouse's unfaithfulness. They went through many months of anger before they were able to fully forgive. Reading the story of Hosea helped them.

May I address a common betrayal experienced among many of you reading this book? This betrayal doesn't involve infidelity with a person in the flesh. Pornography occurs every minute in the US by thousands of men and many leaders. David never personally struggled with this sin, but I have witnessed hundreds destroyed by it. This betrayal is often played down because it's not technically being unfaithful with another human being. THIS IS A LIE! Jesus said that if a man looks on another woman lustfully that it is as if he has actually committed adultery. The Bible states that the eyes are the lamp of the body. When we open a door of darkness and lust through our eye gate we become a slave to sin. Addiction sets in.

Often when a man has been addicted to porn for a long time, he begins to either satisfy himself instead of coming to his wife, or ask her to engage in inappropriate sexual relations. If these acts lose their desired affect, then he begins to look elsewhere for the excitement he craves. Many times a man who has not committed adultery with another person, but has been involved with pornography, is harder to bring to repentance then someone caught in adultery. Many men/women continue to deceive themselves, believing that they haven't broken covenant because they have not had a physical affair. What a sad deception.

How do you begin to heal from wound upon wound, and the ongoing waves that ripple out from this kind of betrayal? NOT ALONE! You begin first by communicating honestly, prayerfully and consistently with the one who betrayed you. You worship together and alone. You pray separately and together. You cry out for help and grace to forgive. You become accountable as a couple to a counselor or minister of healing. If there are no professionals near you, then you choose friends who are willing to walk with you to healing. An intimate circle of friends are invaluable in these situations. Many local churches offer support groups for sexual issues. There are several ministries that now offer weekend or week-long intense ministry for couples or individuals pursuing healing in these broken areas.

Another weapon in our arsenal of forgiveness was using the phrase, "There are reasons for everything but NO EXCUSES." This was a phrase that David introduced to me to that became a cornerstone for moving forward in our healing process. Another familiar quip often quoted is, "hurting people hurt other people." We both faced the reasons for David's betrayal…sexual abuse that led to sexual addiction that led to broken covenants. I am *not* condoning the behavior or approving of it. Yes, hurting people do hurt others — and their own unhealed wounds are usually the reason — BUT there is no explanation that excuses the on-going infliction of pain on others.

I would go often, in my mind to the reasons for David's infidelity in order to cope with my pain. He didn't want to be unfaithful, I would remind myself. He loved me, our family and the Lord. He was trapped by lies in his soul that kept him from receiving the freedom the Lord wanted to bring him. Other truths I spoke to myself were, "Relationships are hard no matter who you are with. Leaving him would leave our children in a "fatherless" household." These thoughts did help me to cope with my own pain, even though they didn't excuse David's behavior.

Learning to recognize the schemes of the enemy was another truth we battled with. Remember the prophetic word preached by David Wilkerson? I would acknowledge that the enemy had been going around seeking whom he could devour. We often get so focused on who hurt us that we forget who our real enemy is! Satan is — not the offender, and not God! We bound the spirit of accusation from operating in us or through us. We reminded ourselves that Satan does not want any marriage to succeed or forgiveness to reign so healing may come! Remember, you will eventually become a weapon in the Master's hand to minister to other wounded couples. David and I would remind ourselves of the greatness of our God by making declarations about who we were and who Jesus was through us.

Again, there are many different types of support available to those walking out of the destruction of infidelity or sexual abuse. I know of countless Christians whose lives have been devastated by all kinds of sexual betrayal: a dad abusing his child, a child abusing other children, a wife being unfaithful with a young man being mentored by her husband, a husband leaving his wife, for another man, and the list goes on. I have personally received the healing touch of God. I have witnessed His faithfulness restore and redeem terrible situations when hearts are submitted to Him, the all-knowing and all-forgiving God. For me personally, it was worth the judgment, pain and struggle I endured to find the joy of release in Jesus.

Don't give up! Let Jesus work out every detail of your life for good.

Idols Fall and Rage Erupts

After David's confession of sin, and our subsequent pathway of restoration, we heard the Lord say we were going to be released from Dallas. We had fulfilled the restoration period of one year, required by our senior pastor after David's confession. Part of the restoration process required that we take a sabbatical and work in the secular arena. We had submitted to this and were healed in many areas. David was still having trouble shaking the shame from his open confession in Dallas, and the Lord had been speaking to us about a move to start over. God was not offering us a chance to run away, but was offering us a move towards newness. We felt the Lord leading us to Colorado Springs.

Leaving our home of twelve years, in Dallas, was a huge decision but it came with tremendous peace. As we prayed, the Lord brought favor and our leadership released us to leave. We had no position or job in Colorado Springs, though Dutch Sheets, our co-worker and close friend, had made it clear he would love for us to be there. He encouraged us that there might be a job opening, leading worship at the church he had begun to pastor, so we packed up and moved in accordance with the things we had been hearing from the Lord. Shortly after arriving there, we were offered a position at Dutch's church. We settled into our home and our mountain town. I was excited for this beautiful new place. I felt renewed inside and was really beginning to heal.

Then a surprise — I found out I was pregnant! We had definitely not planned this! We both thought our family was complete since we hadn't taken any precautions to prevent pregnancy for the previous few years. What a beautiful representation of new beginnings this child would be! Brynne, our third daughter, was born in December of 1993.

Soon after she was born I began having really intense dreams about David. I was dreaming he either died, or I was killing him in the dreams! Just a bit scary! Mind you, everything on the outside was looking great. It had been several years since leaving Dallas. No crisis had occurred. What was wrong with me? I was living in the most beautiful city on earth as far as I was concerned. What was up? I didn't have any desire to freak David out, so I initially stalled in telling him, but the dreams persisted. Finally I went to him and shared that something was surfacing in me. I asked him if I could please go to a counselor because I was experiencing hidden rage in my sleep.

Denial mechanisms are an amazing thing! As I began seeing a Christian counselor it became evident that I had never really dealt with or faced my anger towards David and his unfaithfulness. I had not felt really safe until now to "fall apart." David had been in such intense depression during the previous years in Dallas, that I felt the need to be strong. I had never, before this time, had the opportunity to tell my portion of our story in its entirety to anyone. What a relief to have someone listen and validate my pain and the deep places in me that still were not sure that God accepted me. I saw my counselor for a couple of months and then asked David if we could see her together some.

We went several times. For me, the most important thing about that time was being able to say what I needed to say to him, with a third party supporting me. It was safe. My goal was not to "dig up the past" but to uncover any buried layers in me that were still hurting so that we could be restored. I know that there are varying beliefs in churches out there today, but let me urge you to counsel both separately as well as together. Some of the issues and wounds that you have may not be related to your spouse. Some unresolved issues may have been there for years before you met but your marital conflicts have exacerbated them.

I cannot overemphasize the importance of your sharing with someone all that has transpired in your story. God brings healing just in the verbalizing of it. The Bible says to confess your sins and brokenness one to another that you may be healed. Jesus brings perspective through the individual listening and begins to unlock our hurts and fears so we can receive God's grace.

The counseling process was short but intense for me. The hardest part was just allowing myself to be angry. I don't like anger. I don't like feeling anger. The second most difficult thing about the process was sharing my anger and pain in its raw state, with David. Remember the codependency? It doesn't all go away overnight! Our souls are like an onion with layers upon layers of memories and emotions and levels of healing. Through the counseling process I was reaching a very deep level hidden away in my soul. I had to face that I had still idolized my husband by protecting him from my true emotions. I did not want to bring the past up again, but I had to, in order to become whole.

The problem was I was afraid. I was afraid if I let David see how deeply he'd hurt me, he would leave me. I had always done everything to please him and make the road of our life smooth. Deep down I wondered if I let him see ALL my real feelings and reactions to him and to our marriage, would he leave me? As I faced this fear I entered a new level of release of my husband to God. The dreams stopped!! As I shared my pain with David in those sessions, something happened to the idol in my heart. It fell over. I had been dismantling it for years but it finally came down. I can't explain exactly HOW that happened. Yet in my desire for honesty and hearing truth revealed, God imparted that truth to me in a way I could receive it.

So once again, let me encourage you to get help with the emotional process you are facing. Don't "go it alone." Choose to trust someone and get perspective. Face all that is within you, and I trust that for you, as it did for me, change will begin. When I did, the lies came out, the walls came down, and David and I began to heal at the deepest levels of our souls. We truly began to live in reality in our marriage.

Father, please come swiftly and clearly with Your mercy and Your sword of truth. Uncover lies, hidden anger and pain so that my sister/brother may not be hindered in their walk with You. Holy Spirit come with Your revelation of their own sin and help them to stay focused on what You are saying to them– not pointing their finger in judgment at others. Bring reality to their doorstep if they are living in denial. I release them to You that You would be able to work in their lives. Thank you for Your unending grace and perfect love that is extended to them.

CHAPTER 4

Productive Grieving

G rief is a terrible and wonderful emotion created by God. It's terrible because it's so painful and incomprehensible and wonderful because its expression allows us to heal. Unfortunately, many Christians are afraid of it. It is often misunderstood. I initially suppressed my grief because it was too potentially out of control. Many of us allow ourselves or someone else to grieve, but only on our terms. We determine it can only last so long, or can only look a certain way. Our culture doesn't really allow us to grieve like so many other cultures encourage. I personally experienced many people pushing me to be OK after my Dad's death, and then again after David's betrayal, and subsequent death, in 2002. I have heard scenarios of insensitivity repeatedly, from other's as well — stories of careless comments to those who were in their healing process, such as: "It's time to move on," and "Aren't you done yet?"

We Christians sometimes are the most impatient and out of touch with those who are hurting. I was sometimes insensitive myself before I experienced grief personally. We tend to whip out scriptures to "challenge" one another to "move on in faith." Some well-meaning friends shared a particular verse of scripture with the intent to bless me, but it discouraged me instead. Romans 8:28 says, "For God uses all things to work together for good for those that love Him and are called according to His purpose." After David's death from cancer, that verse was thrown casually at me by people who obviously hadn't walked through deep loss. I know that they honestly thought they were helping me, but their ignorance ended up irritating my wound of loss and betrayal. They weren't in close relationship with me and it was not the time for that scripture to be so carelessly presented. Their sharing these words was like trying to put a little band-aid forcibly on a wound that was bleeding profusely.

In the case of my father's death, that same scripture was a lifeline of encouragement I held onto. It gave me impetus to live. It was hope for a future good to come out of a time of intense pain. Timing is everything! Please, if you are reading this and have not experienced grief, be sensitive and err on the side of caution when exhorting the wounded with scripture. I had to forgive those precious saints to Jesus, and make sure, if at all possible, not to have conversations with them about how I was doing!

Several other believers tried to comfort me with "the Lord will be your husband," shortly after David's passing. I wanted to hit them! I didn't want the Lord to be my husband right then. I wanted my husband — with skin on! I had just walked through four months of hell watching my husband die of lung cancer, while believing for his healing that the Lord had promised us. I didn't have faith for anything, let alone the promise that God was going to my partner! Over the next three years — no surprise here — the Lord did prove to be a wonderful husband who did tangible, hands-on intervention for me. But a few months after someone's death, isn't the appropriate time for that encouragement!

None of the grief process really made sense to me unless I kept looking at it from God's perspective. He ordained that we go through deep pain gradually, and in layers. Grieving takes time. It's never the same for any two people, though its cycles are familiar. I remember some "off the wall things" about the process. After David's death I would be in Walmart and start falling apart in the soup aisle. Why Walmart?? I don't know! But I do know that I have heard the same story from other hurting people. Maybe it's the normalcy of the everyday that Walmart represents. I would yell at myself, "Why can't you fall apart at home or at church?"

My healing process was messy and unpredictable and it was never convenient! I had to go with the proverbial ebb and flow of grief and pain. It truly was like the ocean in its movement and cycles. There was the denial or the "calm ocean" phase. Then there was the anger or the "stormy ocean" phase. Eventually there was acceptance which represented to me the tide coming in and going back out. Because I had walked down the grief road before, I knew how to grieve "good". By that I mean, I knew about "productive grieving." I knew you had to keep moving forward, even if it's only a little progress, as you process your pain. Each time you return to that place of emotion, it's either a bit less intense or of shorter duration. Eventually, one can heal and visit that place or memory, without a tremendous sense of loss.

Unproductive grieving happens when someone stays stuck in the same painful, emotional place or is emotionally shutdown. Because of the circumstance surrounding my dad's death I locked up my pain after he died. This was not just unproductive grieving – but non-existent grieving! I didn't recognize that I had never processed my grief until I was in my thirties. Processing it then was certainly not convenient. Most people around me couldn't understand what I was feeling so many years after his death. When I finally unlocked what I had buried, I vividly began to remember everything I had shut down years before. Here is an excerpt of journaling about what I felt during some of that time.

"The following days and weeks were a blur. I do remember going and saying good-bye to Daddy at the funeral home. I don't know how I can live with the fact that we didn't say good-bye to him before he died. I have constant thoughts of unreality. It's like a dream. I keep thinking I will wake up. Then reality breaks in on my soul and I am in such despair. I don't want anyone to feel bad for me, so when they ask how I am, I say, 'I'm fine'. I'm struggling with feelings that I somehow I caused his death because I told

God I hated my dad and wished he would die, a few weeks before he died. I know it's ludicrous because God doesn't answer those kinds of prayers, but I still feel it's somehow my fault."

As I continued to express my pain to the Lord in prayer, I was able to heal and move on, though it was years later. Once I did, I noticed that my cycles of depression were less and less.

After David's death many of my friends assumed that after the first year of grieving I would be further along than I was in the healing process. In actuality, I had so much to do and so much to cope with the first year that it was hard for me to find time to process my grief. I was dealing with life insurance, financial decisions, death certificates and transferring all our assets and legal documents to my name. I was trying to decide what to with my life and to figure out who I was alone without David and the ministry.

In those first few months after David's death, I also struggled with a very surprising issue. I became tormented by the idea that David was not happy or in heaven. As a strong Christian I knew this was a lie, but I couldn't shake the feeling. I was finally able to recognize that I was trying to connect with him the way we did when he was alive. Impossible! Through our years of battling for healing, I had developed a very keen sense of how he was doing emotionally. We had a very strong soul connection. I went to my pastor, Michael Fletcher, and asked him to lead me through the breaking of this soul tie. It was a process for me to let go of what I had been used to. My connection with David — that sensing — was in such contrast to the empty, unfeeling silence of death. It actually took about a year for this lie to be broken completely in me.

My second year after my husband's death was the most intense for crying and depression, out of the three years I spent in the throes of grief. During that year I was finally able to go to the deep places of pain with God.

I literally had moved my family away to another state where I hardly knew anyone. I felt that if I could be somewhere else I might find the freedom to fully release my emotions. I was still performance oriented enough that I would not face the agony inside me if I stayed at the church where David and I had ministered together. I wanted to display that I trusted God through the whole journey, and not appear too messy. I put so many false expectations on myself and there were others who unconsciously added their own expectations. We held such a public position of leadership that I felt that everyone was watching to see how I would respond. It was a very vulnerable feeling. I felt pressure to hold my head up high and put my best face forward in order to repre- sent what I thought was a godly woman. I also felt strongly in my heart that if I didn't leave the church we had served in, that the people would not move on and embrace the new leader replacing David. As it turned out, the period of time away from the location of his actual death, was the most intense and the most healing I experienced.

It was in my third year of grief that I began writing music to express where I had been emotionally and how I felt during this desert experience. Writing music was a fulfillment of prophetic words I had received many years before. Various prophetic words had been given to me that I would write songs of healing. Little did I know what would be required of me to write those songs! I honestly felt during that season that God only spoke to me a few times. In Psalm 34 it states, "He is near to the broken hearted and saves those who are crushed in spirit." This is a scripture often quoted to hurting individuals, but during grief is usually when God feels the farthest away. I have heard numerous Christian widows express that silence from heaven is a common thread in grieving.

I remember one day during that year that I hit a sudden, surprising low of agony. I went into my basement to wail and cry. I was crying loudly and was afraid my kids would hear me. Let me interject that I believe you should let your children see you cry! They need to see you work through the process. But this day, I was almost beside myself. It was scary. As I sat down in the dark I began wailing to the Lord, "Is there anyone who even knows that I am alive and cares that I am in pain?" Just as I finished my tirade, the phone rang. I don't even know why, but I answered it. A voice on the other end said, "Laurie, are you OK? This is Doug." It was my financial advisor. Now that's a miracle! This was a man that I didn't even have a close friendship with and an analytical man at that! God had reached down and impressed on a human across the country, to call me

—someone with skin on! He will reach out and touch us if we need Him. He is a faithful Savior.

I have long since "finished" the process, but can even now, after five years, still be brought to tears and the sense of deep loss on occasions. My heart still remembers what was lost. Joy does come in the morning and springs do come out of the desert. I actually jumped out of an airplane (with a parachute!) from 14,000 feet, to mark the beginning of moving forward. I was ready to "declare" that new life had begun and that I wasn't going to live in the memory of David's death. I have stated many times in the past few years that I hate the grief process, but God has encouraged me with this word from Exodus 23: 30-31, "I will not drive them out in a single year, that the land may not become desolate and the beasts of the field become too numerous for you. I will drive them out before you little by little until you become fruitful and take possession of the land." Normally this scripture is used to minister deliverance and hope in the process of sanctification. But the Holy Spirit has brought immeasurable comfort from it while I endured the long grief process. I wasn't crazy! God intended it to take awhile. That was my comfort.

The grief process takes a different amount of time for every individual who goes through it, depending on the situation and the proximity of the relationship to you. For example, was it your sibling, mom, grandparent or your spouse who died? Your personality type, and the level of intimacy that was in your relationship with that individual or situation, affects the length of the process as well. How long it takes to heal is affected by our temperament, by whether we have to change our work situation, financial issues and many other factors. It is a process that cannot be predicted or predetermined! I used to refer to my intense time of grieving as the "Yo-yo Sisterhood Club" or the "Half-eimer's Club" (Not to be mistaken with Alzheimer's as I only lost half my brain.) So please have patience with yourself. Don't give up in the process. Your brain function will be restored. You will find new relationships.

Father, please come near my friend as he/she is healing from their loss. Give them grace and patience with themselves for the grief process. Help them to continue to move forward through their pain towards You. Bring people alongside them that will weep with them and comfort them. Restore all that has been lost and cause their latter days to be greater than their former days. In Jesus' name.

CHAPTER 5

Carrying the Shame

Recently I was talking with a friend who was betrayed by her husband with moral failure and we were discussing the difference between shame and guilt. As we looked at the two very similar emotions, there was a definite distinction between them. Guilt is how we feel about what we have done. Shame is from an internal place and expresses how we see ourselves and what we believe about who we are. Shame basically says there is something wrong with me. Both can be debilitating, but shame can destroy us.

As we shared our stories, we realized we both carried shame. Both of us had experienced reproach from the church as well. (I would describe reproach as guilt from an external source.) This reproach from people made us feel that we had somehow contributed to our husband's moral failures. Shame enveloped our hearts saying there must be something unlovely or wrong with us that our husbands would want someone else, especially another man.

Reproach was particularly directed at my friend because she didn't share publicly the details of her husband's sin, so people blamed her for their breakup. How horrible to be blamed for someone else's choices. Another friend experienced reproach from her church because she was overweight and people inferred that it was her fault that her husband was unfaithful! Joy was a dear friend whose husband was very publicly unfaithful to her through homosexuality. She fought to come out from under the lie of shame for almost four years. It almost destroyed her. These are the kinds of stories that made me all the more driven to prove that I was the perfect wife, so that all would know I was not at fault.

One reason shame can take such a hold on an individual, is that it isolates you. You continually hear the voice of shame over the voice of acceptance or reason. I have talked to numerous men and women who have expressed similar feelings of carrying someone else's shame. Jesus is the only one that can carry someone else's shame. Jesus is qualified to carry our shame because He defeated sin and all its power through His shed blood on the cross. He was called to this purpose. We, however, are not called to carry shame, neither our own nor that of another. When we try to do it, it weighs us down and breaks our back. Thinking that I have to carry someone else's shame is a debilitating lie of the enemy. Betsy and Chester Kylstra have a powerful teaching in their book, "An Integrated, Biblical Approach to Healing." They write of how shame, fear, and control often work together to create bondages in a person's life. If you struggle with shame I highly recommend you read it.

Staying in bondage to shame and all of its lies will keep us from wholeness and freedom. I experienced both shame and healing from the public confession that David and I went through in Dallas over his moral indiscretion. He was not "caught" in his sin, but had come to me and to the elders of the church where we ministered as worship leaders. He poured out his heart in repentance. He uncovered himself in sorrow for the sin that had ensnared him. Although most of our congregation responded with loving forgiveness and support, I felt as if I had done something wrong myself. David was in the middle of another Integrity Hosanna recording at the time of his confession and we were asked to halt it due to his moral failure. We both felt shame every time we encountered any of Integrity's staff for several years after that.

I personally carried David's shame and my own, for over two years. I felt the weight of the accusation, "I am dirty and have done something that is displeasing to the Lord". I felt ostracized by many other Christians after the initial outpouring of love and acceptance. Everything changed in our everyday lives as we embarked on a sabbatical from ministry and eventually worked in the marketplace instead of the church. None of the flow of life was the same. We both felt like we had been abandoned on an island of isolation and pain.

During this struggle with shame I believed a lie that I had done something to displease the Lord. I had to stand up with my husband and be a part of his brokenness in front of the world. Surely, I had some hidden awful thing wrong with me! Well, the truth is that I did have something wrong with me. It's called sin! I am not being religious. The doorway out of shame for me was the revelation of *my own sinfulness.* I had to see that apart from Christ I was dirty, filthy, and broken, just as my husband was broken *–and not just by his homosexual sin.*

I had been trapped in a cycle of religious mindsets that spoke to me saying I was not the guilty one because I had not been unfaithful. I was the good girl. I had forgiven him. But the truth is — but for the grace of God there I went. All I needed were the right circumstances and it would be me committing sexual sin with someone instead of David. I already had lied. I had gossiped and the Bible is clear that gossip is like murdering someone. The truth is that sin is in all of us. Let's level the playing field of sin. God hates lying. God hates homosexuality. God hates gossip. God hates sin in every form. When I finally got the revelation – and it was just that – I was devastated by what I saw in myself. It was the beginning of the end for shame in my soul. The enemy said I was a broken sinner and dirty. I agreed...... *BUT - I am redeemed from the pit by his grace and mercy!!! His blood has cleansed me*! The power of this hidden lie being exposed began setting my mind free.

We must continually come before the face of Jesus and see who we are without Him. We must live in the revelation that we are nothing apart from Him. This revelation brings a grace to walk out the healing process because we are not pointing the finger at our offender. We are spotlighting ourselves. The Holy Spirit is always interested in the condition of my heart. When He's communicating with me, He is looking to change my perspective first. The Bible clearly portrays this basic truth over and over. Coincidentally, the same day I received this revelation of my sin, David received the same revelation of his sinfulness and his soul began its healing journey as well. We were in separate places, in our cars, of all places! God knew that we both had to get our eyes on Him and Him alone, to make it.

May I challenge you with something? If you have been shamed through your own sin or someone's sin against you, then go after the shame to destroy it! Break its back with a vengeance. If shame is left in your souls, it is a doorway of weakness through which the enemy can enter. Shame blocks the power of Christ's resurrection from being experienced in our lives. Sanctification in Him is a process of "positional truth" becoming "absorbed, experienced truth." Shame in our souls will stop the truth from becoming a revelation of freedom to us. I am convinced that if shame isn't dealt with that you are giving the enemy permission to walk right into your life. I'm sure of this consequence of shame because of what I shared from the scriptures earlier, and for another reason — my precious husband's death.

About a month and a half before David died, an intercessor in our church had a dream about him. She submitted her dream to the church leadership and was released to send it to us. It was a dream about shame. She knew little about the details of our lives or struggles. The dream was a picture of a bird pecking with its beak at David's liver. The bird's name was SHAME. When I read the dream to David, I asked him if it was true. He said "Yes, I am still struggling with shame about who I am and what I've done." After all the grace and freedom that he had begun to experience in his relationship with the Father, he still felt unclean in the deepest part of his soul.

Immediately, I was deeply concerned. I knew it was a doorway for the cancer to hold onto. I am NOT saying that the devil stole David from this world. I am saying that I believe God took him out of evil days ahead to keep him in peace. (Paraphrase of Isaiah 51:2.) There were literally thousands of Christians praying and fasting for his healing. We had heard the Lord say He would heal him. David was whole and strong in so many areas, but there was a doorway open to future brokenness lingering in his soul. When we agree with lies of the enemy it gives Satan permission or legal rights to attack us. I believe the Father heard David's cry for righteousness and holiness, and preserved him by taking him at his strongest. He had fought long and hard for his liberty in Jesus. He is now able to do what was always in his heart to do: Worship Jesus in purity and holiness and focus on Him because He is worthy!

In the areas of both physical and sexual abuse, guilt usually drives the responses of the abused person. Guilt says, "You made wrong choices that caused this to happen," and, "it's your fault." These accusations that produce feelings of guilt often come in with rape or molestation. "If I hadn't gone there, then this wouldn't have happened." "If I had done something differently, then he wouldn't have hit me." The list goes on and on.

The Bible says that we are all foolish should covet being wise. It's a righteous goal to do and say the right things — HOWEVER — when we blow it, out of ignorance or rebellion, there is still redemption through His blood. The Bible clearly says in I John 1:9, "If we confess our sins, He is faithful and just to forgive us our sins and to cleanse us from all unrighteousness." We have to let go of the whip that we use against ourselves and receive His redemption in our situation.

Remember what it's like as a parent to watch your child make a foolish mistake? Your heart is just broken. Is there anything but compassion there as a parent? You wish you could rewind the tape. If you are not a parent, remember a time when you watched someone you cared about choose to do something that was foolish. Do you remember what was in your heart towards them? Was it sorrow, or maybe compassion? If we, as earthly children of God and sinners, feel those kinds of merciful feelings, how much more does your heavenly Father and Redeemer? So I encourage you to repent of believing the lie that you are "unforgivable" and receive His cleansing from your shame. Don't allow the enemy to ensnare you any longer through fear and shame.

Father, I pray in the precious name of Jesus for the oil of Your grace to be poured into and onto my precious sister or brother. Let the bright light of Your truth envelop them and dispel every vestige of darkness that has lied to them about who they are. You say we are your precious children and you loved us enough to die for us and carry our shame. Your Word says You delight in us. Help them to receive this truth. Empower my sister/brother to break the back of shame by believing Your word.

CHAPTER 6

The Identity Piece

As I mentioned earlier, because of what sin does to our souls, we end up with distorted truths in the center of them. We function so much out of our identity — how we see ourselves, how we view God, how we believe that He sees us and, how we view others. I liken it to a mirror in which, when it's unbroken, we see a clear reflection of ourselves and others. When it's shattered and we look into it, or hold it out to view others, all kinds of distortions are present with whole chunks missing. Paraphrased the Bible says that we behold Jesus now in a mirror dimly, and that we know in part now, but that we will know Him fully when we see Him. (I Corinthians 13:12)

To find true freedom from our shattered perspectives we must go backwards in our memories by the leading of the Holy Spirit to see where we formulated the ungodly beliefs that now distort our identity. Not only must we examine what we have learned with our minds (head knowledge,) but we must seek for understanding in our hearts about what we've absorbed from our life experiences.

Romans 12:2 paraphrased, says that we need to renew our minds so we can be transformed. When we submit to the Holy Spirit and His revelatory power, we can receive God's divine perspective on the events in our lives. Part of sanctification, is this process of allowing the Holy Spirit to uncover lies we have falsely believed from our experiences. Misinterpretations of our experiences lead to false perceptions. In other words, we sometimes build our lives on lies without even realizing it. As we allow the Holy Spirit to lead us, He uncovers the lies and we are able to receive truth through the scriptures, through good teaching, and through His revelation. Once we have recognized the truth, we become transformed as Romans 12:2 promises. The false belief system comes down and the foundation of our lives is restructured according to the truth. When our identity is not wholly founded in Christ and we still have fractured belief systems, our effectiveness is limited when it comes to being a conduit for God, or receiving from Him.

The Bible says in Colossians that we are made complete in Him. He is the head of the body and we are His temple. Complete, according to Webster's Dictionary means, "to make whole, full, to fill up or perfect – the inclusion of all that is needed for." Colossians 2:15-17 says, that essentially, "from Him, through Him and to Him are all things." Psalm 139 declares that we are "fearfully and wonderfully made" by God in our mother's womb. We confess that His words are truth, but unfortunately because of sin, wounds and tragedy, we become unsure of their reality in our lives. We begin to see God with distortion and doubt who He says He is, or who He says we are. Other Christian teachers refer to this kind of distortion as an ungodly belief system or a lie. I've used these terms in this book as well.

An illustration would be helpful. I lived for years and years with a huge piece of my identity missing – my daddy piece. Because my dad died so suddenly and we were not encouraged to grieve fully, I shut down my memories of life with my dad and promptly forgot most of my childhood. I dissociated from the pain and loss and locked my emotions away. The lie I took on was that I could never expect life to happen to the fullest. I unconsciously believed that abandonment or tragedy was always around the corner.

On the day my dad died, my uncle, a Methodist pastor, very lovingly quoted Romans 8:28, "All things work together for good for those that love God and are called according to His purpose." This is God's word, but in my brokenness I heard this in a warped way, and I began unconsciously living in expectation of crisis, believing that was how God had to teach me. I was just that much of a "hard head!" God just had to "lay it on me" to get my attention. Wow – what strange things we can believe from our warped perceptions.

That day, I also began to believe that my heart would remain empty and dissatisfied without a dad. Thus I began to look for affection and camaraderie with men to try and fill that empty place in my soul.

I wasn't sleeping with anyone, but I certainly was flirting with guys and wanting their affection physically. I played very dangerous games and it was only the Lord's grace as a Father to me that kept me from being raped or harmed sexually.

A strong performance mentality has also driven me for years. I tried to do everything to please God and man so that I would be loved. I was always looking for the approval of people. I wanted to please everyone. I applied this same mindset with David. I thought that if I did all the right things, then he would love me. If I learned to fold the underwear the correct way and hang the clothes up in an organized manner, and kept the house spotless, and had all the right responses then he would love me more. Well guess what? I am supposed to please GOD! I had to go back to the places I formed these lies and allow the Holy Spirit to begin to replace them with His truth. When we don't replace lies we have believed with God's perspective, they continue to influence and drive our attitudes and behaviors for years to come.

Sometimes, they even cause us to have blocked hearing. Has anyone ever complimented you and you "didn't receive it" because of the way you felt you looked? I recently had a prophetic word sent to me that had been spoken over me eighteen years ago. It was a direct answer to a prayer I had cried out to God. During the last four years. I had doubted that I still had a calling to ministry. I kept asking God to show me clearly what He had planned for my life. A friend had found a CD of a personal prophecy, given to me, in his archives and decided to send it to me. As

I listened to it, I couldn't remember EVER hearing it! There was a second word on the CD to my son, Collin, and guess what? I remembered *that* word! Can you figure out one of the things the Lord had said to me?? It was "Laurie, you are a Jeremiah, **called from the womb** to speak forth my prophetic word." HELLO?! Where was I when that word was given? I was "straight arming" God's word to me because of my own wounds at the time. I had just found out that David had been unfaithful to me right after Collin's birth, and I couldn't believe in a future because I was in so much pain. The Lord had answered my current question years before. Are you rejecting the very thing that God is trying to give you because of your judgments about how it's being delivered or because of your distorted beliefs?

One of my identity deceptions had to do with how I saw myself. Since I've been widowed I have not been asked out much by men. I have been out with a few men, but at my instigation. So I began to be sucked into the lie that there was something wrong with me and I was unattractive. The Holy Spirit saw that lie coming though, and reminded me that I had prayed for God to keep me safe from my own mechanisms in regard to relationships. He had been answering my prayer!

My initial response to not being asked out by men was an old habit of response left over from my teenage years. Back then if no one asked you out you were considered unlovely and unwanted. What a distortion of truth! I went to a friend and we prayed and breakthrough came to me. I had not been faced with these issues for a long time since I'd been married for twenty-one years. Now as my life changed, after David's death I was suddenly reverting to the only other time I had been single — to an old mindset. Have you been there? Are you getting the picture? We can believe mistruths at any age and arrive at them from just about any circumstance.

Ask the Holy Spirit to highlight any areas that are ensnared by your false belief systems. I recently saw one in my life that has been there for years! It was keeping me from standing my ground when confrontation occurred. I had been aware of the behavior pattern before, especially with those in authority, but I had no idea it was rooted in a lie deep in my soul.

Years ago I was accused of using some inappropriate language at my job at a Christian school. The woman who was accusing me called a meeting with leadership of my church. To make a long story short, my accuser wouldn't believe I hadn't said what they thought I'd said. I apologized and explained that she must have misunderstood me, to no avail. The leader who was meeting with us finally said to me, "Laurie, you are going to have to take the low road and apologize as if you did it." Now the concept of maturity and humility are biblical in that statement, but I took it into my soul in a twisted way. I unconsciously decided that I could not stand up for myself, even if I knew I was right. To back down was a more righteous response. Yikes! Crazy, but it's what happened inside me. I lived out of that decision until recently. The cycle had been presenting itself again. I could not fire a workman that was not doing the job he was hired for. Once I recognized and repented for believing the falsehood, I immediately was able to fire the man and move on.

Another skewed identity piece that I still struggle with today is eating. Instead of looking to the Lord to fill me, I eat to numb my pain, to soothe my loneliness or to deal with stress. I've tried "breaking up with this boyfriend" and I just keep running back to him! As a teen and young adult, no one really knew the food addictions I struggled with, because I never allowed myself to gain more than ten pounds and hid my overeating from the public eye. It was a huge crutch and idol in my life not only after my father died, but also after David's death. I would eat to comfort myself, to feel better, and to numb my pain and agitation. I would treat myself to food because I couldn't have physical contact, comfort or intimacy.

All I have to do is look around to know I am not the only one practicing this mechanism of coping. It's evident by our clothes size, that the American church as a whole struggles with the idolatry of food and this response to pain and stress. Remember the scripture I shared at the beginning of this chapter? Who are you in Christ? You are complete in Him, and so am I. Eating to complete ourselves is not what He ordained for life and godliness! Now when I feel the urge to indulge, I try to worship, or fill my hands with service.

I have one more personal story to share in regards to broken identity places in my soul. It's a story about how I wasted a lot of energy living in shame. All my life I hated my chin. I inherited from my mom's family a loose skin chin. I called it a turkey gobbler chin! I hated my profile and I hated the fact that everyone always knew when I put on weight, as it showed there first. Before David died we talked about getting my chin tucked. I didn't want to look younger. I just wanted the chin gone. So after his death I started thinking about it again. I waffled back and forth for a couple of years over whether to do it. I researched the surgery and didn't like the price tag I saw, so I made an unthinking commitment: I would do it if I built an orphanage. Now I said this very jokingly to family and friends. Well, guess what? I helped build an orphanage in Sri Lanka. I began looking at options again. I had basically let go of the idea of plastic surgery, when a friend called to tell me that she had found a procedure where I wouldn't have to go under anesthesia. I would only miss two days of work and the cost was much cheaper. I began considering it and praying about it.

Before I go any further, let me say that I am, neither condoning, nor condemning plastic surgery. (Remember, I had already had my breast size surgically reduced.) However, for me this was a decision made out of a skewed view of myself and I want to keep you from going where I did! I researched the procedure, so I thought, and began waiting to have the surgery. The first date scheduled was delayed. The second time, we scheduled the surgery my blood pressure, which is always low, was high. I felt this fog-horn warning going off inside of me, but forged on anyway.

The surgery was to have lasted less than an hour. Since I was awake during the procedure, I had begun to feel my face swell. It felt like it had been FOREVER, so I asked what time it was. The doctor indicated it had been two-plus hours since the instigation of the procedure! I asked why it was taking so long, starting to panic, and he replied there was a lot of bleeding. Let me give you the short version. After the surgery I was black and blue from my temples to my collar bone. I was in agony. I had incisions rip open and other complications. I missed two weeks of work. After wanting the surgery to be kept a secret, everyone ended up knowing about it, because of all the complications.

What happened to my soul is the worst part. I began to believe that I was unable to hear God's voice and that He was disappointed in me because I had not heeded His warning. The resulting uncertainty and insecurity led to a very tumultuous year of indecision. I was paralyzed by shame. I felt I'd made a horrible mistake. To top it off, I wasn't in the least bit happy with the procedure or the results. Months later, people were telling me that I looked so young and I was mortified! I liked the way I looked before! I didn't want to be a "fake" younger! I couldn't receive any compliments by then.

A year passed and one day I decided that I needed to be able to tell my story. The problem was I couldn't talk about it because I was bound by shame. So I went after the shame and received prayer. The Holy Spirit took me in my mind to the day of surgery, and showed me a huge angel spread over the top of my body during the procedure. Jesus was standing by my bed and weeping. He was not weeping because I had been an idiot, but because I had suffered and could have died. He preserved my life. The truth! It was the opposite of what the enemy had been speaking to me.

My encouragement to you is to accept yourself the way you were created, but if you have made unwise choices or decisions you are not proud of, give them to Jesus and accept that we all make mistakes. He wants to redeem all things in our lives, but we have to *let* Him. He wants to use all things for His glory, but we have to *let* Him. Don't leave any foothold for the enemy by not fully allowing the Holy Spirit to set you free from shame. I am free of it today, not because of what I've done, but because of Whose I am. Receiving this truth is where freedom lies.

Are you able to see any cycles present in your life, which produce inappropriate responses that seem to be driven by something, lurking underneath? The broken identity pieces we all struggle with must be healed before we can be an effective conduit for His power and love. We won't deliver our potential impact in the kingdom of God in our ordained sphere of influence, when we function out of a distorted perspective of who God is. Our efforts to show His unconditional love are impaired when we have skewed views of who He is and who we are or are not. Are you willing to let Jesus put back together the fractured belief systems you have? Can you daily ask for the renewing of your mind and the uncovering of the places in your soul that you have

built faulty beliefs about yourself or Him? Will you
say to yourself what He says about you?

Let me close with you this powerful poem about
who we are, by my friend Gabriel Gause.

"Reflection"

Sitting at the river bank on a warm summer
  day
the sun is glistening like the sparkling beauty
  of diamonds.
In the still and peaceful calm, trees on the
  other side of the river bed
  are casting their reflections on the water.
Like the mirror, mirror on the wall a mirror
  image of them all
  in the sparkling glory of the light.
Oh, but suddenly the rippling effect of the
  waves created by the wind's adversities,
  troubles and the crippling memories of
  past sins,
  changed the beautiful image once so pure
  and innocent
  into one that is marred.
The slim, tall pines, in distorted view, now
  slithering snakes driven by the pain
  of false image heartbreaks.
Mirror, mirror on the wall why are you lying
  to them all?
All the trees planted by the streams were
  meant to prosper and fulfill their dreams.

Mirror, mirror on the wall, no more, that's it,
I hear the call!
Mirror, image of the Word, let it be seen and
let it be heard!
He for me has been nail scarred, my image
now, no longer marred.
Mirror, image of the Word let it be seen and
let it be heard
A descendant of royal lineage – I am created
in His Image!

Father, in the name of Jesus, I ask that you would take my brother or sister and bring your revelatory truth to them about the different lies they have believed about themselves and You. Answer their cry for wholeness, specifically, and show them where the broken places have kept them from receiving your blessing. Heal the shattered, hidden places of their souls and bring clarity to their clouded judgments. Give them eyes to see and ears to hear how YOU perceive them. Write Psalm 139 on their hearts, that they are fearfully and wonderfully made.

CHAPTER 7

The Devil Doesn't Play Fair – Generational Iniquity Patterns

In Exodus 20:5 the Bible says that the iniquities of the fathers are passed down to the third and fourth generations until a sacrifice has been made. Jesus was the sacrifice provided to break that curse. However, as you may know, we need to appropriate the truth for it to be activated or released in us. The basic concept, with generational curses or family patterns of iniquity, is we need to appropriate Christ's provision through repentance, forgiveness and the breaking of curses that are passed down from generation to generation of a family line. I shared in a previous chapter Exodus 23:29-31. God is basically saying that we will gain freedom and deliverance a bit at a time. Remember the "little by little, *until*" part? Until we are strong, able and aware! This can apply to the progression of the sanctification process in our lives. The Lord is saying that deliverance and freedom are a process in our lives and we need to be patient! If the Lord brought our deliverance too quickly we would not be able to maintain it.

David and I had received and appropriated this teaching when we decided to plan a family. Knowing our family histories and wanting to be good stewards of righteousness, we began to fast and pray for the children we would have. We understood that we would have to deliberately close the doors on the sin patterns in our families through prayer in order to take back the legal ground that the enemy had held through past generations' sin. One of the easiest ways to find out your family's history, even if you are unable to get them to talk about it, is to look at your own behaviors! Look at your immediate family's cycles and "weirdness". Alcoholism, sexual abuse, anger, obsessive behaviors, prolific infirmities, lying, accidents and financial loss are some examples of patterns that can run in families due to inheriting generational iniquities. You don't have to be Sherlock Holmes to figure out the areas in which the enemy has and will come after you and your children! He's pretty predictable.

We knew the enemy would come after some of our kids with sexual sin and either religious or occult ideologies because of behavior patterns we saw in our families! The occult issues were related to my grandfather being a Mason. For those of you unfamiliar with Freemasonry, it has occult associations because of its deceptive nature, (it's a secret society), and because of some of the blood covenants involved in Masonic rituals. My maternal grandfather had been a 33rd level Mason, so this opened doors to many curses because of the evil oaths made by him. To close doorways open to darkness through these curses, David and I made specific, declarations of freedom through prayer, and confessions of all kinds of perversions and compulsions. Ongoing prayer was done in combination with deliverance by bringing all our families' past iniquities under the blood of Jesus. I had very little understanding at that time, of the war we were already in. I must say here how thankful and amazed I am at how the Father led us to incredible men and women of God, who deposited sound doctrine and truth in us. Their teaching and support enabled us to understand the path we needed to walk in order to succeed. We would never have made it without the understanding and wisdom they imparted to us.

Soon after finding out we were pregnant, we began receiving all kinds of prophetic words that we were having a boy. Of course, we wanted a first-born male to help bring freedom to the generations to come. We felt it was important to have a male child to war against the perversion that had existed in David's generational line. History has shown through many cultures the blessing that is on the firstborn male child. A greater emphasis of authority, inheritance and favor is often associated with the male. Remember the story of Esau and Jacob and the deception involved in attaining the inheritance that was due the firstborn? Well, spring of 1984 arrived and so did our *daughter*!! We were so shocked! We quickly recovered and began enjoying *her*!

As I mentioned in an earlier chapter, she was an adorable, but very serious baby. It was not until several years later that I began to get a clue about the evil plans of destruction that the enemy had already unleashed on her as our firstborn. When she was still a toddler, she began to exhibit some behaviors that were not "normal" for one so little. She was intensely interested in her private parts. We began gently trying to distract her and to teach simple concepts about honoring God and her body. Through the years we presented, in a very safe manner, instruction on inappropriate touch and strangers, etc. She seemed to be doing better with her fascination, but something just didn't feel right to me. I would run to God in prayer with the thoughts I was having. "God we've prayed against perversion. We've taught her self-protection. We've declared freedom. We've made it safe for her to talk to us if anything happened to her, so what is going on?" As she got older I began to wonder if anyone had ever touched her inappropriately. When asked, she denied anything. We were very careful about who she was with, who babysat her and who she played with, so I just chalked it up to my paranoid imagination.

Brooke came to accept Jesus as her Savior and was blossoming into a lovely young girl who was exceptional in her behavior and obedience. One day I heard the Holy Spirit say, "Ask Brooke again about someone abusing her." I obeyed but to no avail. Brooke denied that anything had ever happened. A year went by and the Holy Spirit said to ask her again. I did. She said no again. As you can imagine by this time, I was absolutely sure I was a crazy mom who was making her daughter think about things she shouldn't be thinking about at her age.

More time passed. We had just moved to Colorado Springs starting fresh after David's restoration process in Dallas. One morning, I again heard the Holy Spirit say to ask Brooke the same question. The night before I had been in a deep place of repentance over some issues of forgiveness towards my own mom, and had really gotten a breakthrough. Listen up! This is so important! I believe that *the next event that occurred would not have happened, had I not released forgiveness towards my mom*!

This time when the Holy Spirit spoke I argued back. "You cannot be serious?! What are you thinking? I have already asked over and over!" He was just as insistent right back at me. "ASK HER!" So into her bedroom we went. I asked the same question, the same way, prefaced with how much I loved her and assuring her she wouldn't get in trouble. This time she looked at me, burst into tears and said yes. I was totally blown away. Then the floodgates broke and she began pouring out her confession and shame of children in the neighborhood introducing her to all kinds of sexual things for the past few years. We eventually found out an adult from our church had approached her physically as well.

I was furious with God! I ran into the closet and started sobbing and shouting. "HOW, could YOU let this happen??! We've prayed, we've fasted, we've done all we know to do to protect her! WHY, God??" In the silence after my explosion of pain, I heard the Lord as clearly as if He was sitting next to me, "Laurie, you are in a war and the devil doesn't play fair!" Revelation! He then began to confront the deception I had pacified myself with: If I prayed and made declarations over generational stuff then it was all taken care of and my children wouldn't be attacked in those areas. How foolish of me. I was suddenly shaken into awareness of the spirit world and the war I was in.

That day changed my prayer life forever, as well as how I approached my children's education of the world. David and I prayed together about how we were going to walk with our children on their paths of destiny from here on out. Would we live in fear? Would we allow sleepovers? Would we use babysitters? Where would we draw the boundaries in order to protect our kids in the future? David and I realized that we would have to be alert in these areas of family weakness until the generations after us were walking free. Freedom has happened in our children progressively and completely. The journey to healing was not without mishap, but our daughter is now happily married and stayed pure with her fiancé until marriage.

Brooke, as our firstborn, was also hit with the spirit of infirmity. None of my other children have had such a battle. I personally had struggled with this spirit and stood in faith for years against it in my body, before the key of revelation came with regards to curses of sickness through Freemasonry. I have continually encouraged Brooke to rise up and war with the word against the curse the enemy has hit her with in this area. The enemy has not taken David's and my declarations lightly. We declared that the generations to come would walk free of these sins and curses. Satan doesn't take our word for it, but will always challenge our proclamations! Be prepared in prayer and with wisdom and discernment.

The next place of "warring through" came with the advent of my pregnancy with my second daughter, Heather. Brooke was just six months old when we discovered I was pregnant again. What a shock! I was still breastfeeding Brooke, and in no way wanted another baby just yet. I had only just begun to deal with my pain over David's infidelities. I cried out to God in desperation for Him to cause my heart to change. I was a Christian! I wasn't supposed to be upset at the idea of new life given by God! But I was! I cried out to Him for many months and He took me through gradual steps of repentance and healing in my heart so that I could trust Him with the little one coming.

After Heather was born I suspected from her interactions with me that I had damaged her heart with my rejection before her birth. She was a daddy's girl all the way. She was also our whiny child and everything seemed to upset her. She never saw the good in things. Her cup was ½ empty – not ½ full! I began to pray and repent of the negative emotions I'd felt while she was developing, I asked the Lord to give me wisdom and hope. One day He spoke to me and said, "Heather will be a great joy to you in her teen years." I hung on to that promise with desperation.

Suddenly, one day when Heather was four or five years old, she looked up at me and said, "Mommy – I love daddy more than you." After my initial surprise, I responded, "Yes honey, I know, but that doesn't make mommy love you any less, and I love you no matter what." I immediately felt such a peace flood over me and thanked God for His wisdom in giving me a wise response for her.

From that day forward Heather began to let me into her heart in a new way. As with Brooke, we prayed at different stages of her life for her continued healing of the immature ways that we had responded to her or raised her. As the Lord met her and healed her little heart from my rejection of her in the womb, she changed dramatically in her outlook on life. She became a very positive, confident young woman in her teenage years. She was an incredible blessing of joy and stability, just as God had promised me. Heather was never attacked by the enemy physically through infirmity, or sexuality. But she, like any Christian, has had to stand against iniquity patterns in her life such as religious mindsets associated more with my side of the family.

I used to say to David that I wished we had known the right responses and actions to take before damage was done to our children, but the truth is that they would not be who the Lord planned them to be without going through everything they have experienced. We are all in a process and the damaging things that happen to us, when placed in His mighty hands, will be used to make us completely unique in Him.

We became pregnant with our third child. I wasn't ill with this one like the girls, but I felt something was wrong from the beginning. I didn't know if the enemy was torturing me in my mind with lies, or if there was truth in the feelings I was having deep down inside. But at my fourth month checkup my feelings were proven. The baby was dead inside me and had stopped growing three weeks before. Let me interject here that we as women so often second guess ourselves, particularly when it comes to things we sense. I have learned through the years not to rationalize about the thoughts that come, but to PRAY and keep praying until confirmation comes or a release. I went into labor a few days later and delivered my precious baby into Jesus' arms. David and I both grieved for a period of time, but I was able to release that child into the Lord's arms with much grace.

Within several years I was pregnant again. We were hoping for the son that would help break the generational curses of perversion. A boy, to David also meant that God's mercy had fully been poured out on him. Our prayers were answered and Collin was born. He was at that time, and is, the only male grandchild on the Morris side. The Lord gave us a word that Collin was born with a sword in his hand to ram up the family line of curses. He certainly has been a unique young man who does not follow the crowd. He has already had to war against the iniquity patterns of sexual sin and is winning. The enemy presented some opportunities for exposure to pornography when he was young (and believe me –

we were careful!) and then immediately after his dad died. How blatant! He's already had young women try and seduce him. He has a strong call on his life for worship and leadership, and he recognizes that he will have to war and stand against onslaught in these areas. I keep encouraging him that he is blessed as he already knows part of the enemy's plan of attack against him!

The next major blip in the panorama of life relating to iniquity patterns came with my youngest daughter Brynne's birth. I knew when she was born that something wasn't "right". Within hours, my doctor approached us with the news that she was born with congenital hip dysplasia. Her hip sockets were not fully formed. My heart sank initially, and then rose up in adamancy….she was going to be healed! I was not going to stand for the iniquity pattern of infirmity that I had fought so hard to break to have a victory in my daughter.

We had fought through many issues of robbery and sickness invoked by the freemason vows my grandfather participated in. I was so focused on Brynne being healed, that I pushed aside the whispers in my heart saying there was more to this diagnosis then met the eye. Two weeks after her birth, after the initial x-rays and instructions on how to wrap her diaper for therapy, we returned to the specialist's office. He came into our room and looking flustered said, "What have you been doing to her?" I very nervously replied, "Putting her diaper on her like you told us…and praying." He then, very red-faced and obviously perplexed, began to show us her x-rays.

She now had fully formed hip sockets!! The nurses were all stirred up and he definitely did not know what to say! We were in shock! How do you like that for faith??? She was healed – hallelujah!! No therapy needed. No brace needed. WOW! Finally we were seeing a documented instant, miraculous event in the Morris household! We were ecstatic!

In the ensuing weeks we testified over and over again of God's power touching her. Cindy Jacobs wrote about her healing in one of her articles. This made it all the more confusing when as the months passed by, it was evident that Brynne had some emotional and physical issues going on. She exhibited violent behavior at times. She hardly slept at all, and cried and screamed for most of every day. On average, the first year of her life, she cried five plus hours a day. As she got older, she would not, and could not, sleep unless she was holding my hand and she had horrible night terrors regardless. She actually slept with David and me for years as she would not sleep alone. We eventually made a little pallet for her by our bed, instead of getting up and down with her all night long. For four long years I don't remember sleeping without multiple interruptions nightly. We prayed and prayed for deliverance and healing.

I finally had to quit nursing her when the doctor said she was allergic to my milk. I thought it had to be something I was eating. We went through a stage where we wondered if she had demons because the fits were so severe! She was also showing signs of autism. She would bang her head on the wall or floor, stare blankly at people for periods of time, and sometimes would not respond to people at all. As she began learning words, she exhibited severe echolalia (repetitive speech). Once out of the toddler phase, she had a compulsive need for socialization. We asked God how and why would He do a creative miracle in her a body, yet not touch the pathways of her brain and heal her condition. He didn't answer us and I don't know the answer myself. What I do know, is that the very disability that caused her to struggle with multiple areas of learning also protected her from a devastating event.

When we were about to move from Colorado to start working in a church in North Carolina, we found out a boy in the neighborhood had been exposing himself to Brynne. He was much older. I had seen the young man before and felt uncomfortable around him. I had instructed my kids to never play around him or let Brynne be near him. Unfortunately the enemy was sneaky in spite of my caution. My pain and rage were only mollified minutely when we discovered that the exposure appeared to not have affected her the way it would most little girls. The police and the counselors were convinced that her detachment emotionally —related to her mild autism— had protected her from undue emotional scarring. That was then, and today I can attest to that fact. Now a young teenager, she appears to have no lasting scars from this occurrence. Thanks be to God!

The last thirteen years have been very faith building for me as I have walked with Brynne through all kinds of therapy to help her brain integrate and function better. She finally was diagnosed, after much genetic testing, with Pervasive Developmental Delay (PDD) and Sensory Integration Disorder (SIDS). This is a blanket diagnosis that covers the various, multiple learning development issues she struggles with such as dysgraphia, forms of dyslexia and language processing disorders. Trusting God, to teach me how to help Brynne reach her potential hasn't just been tiring, but exciting as well! Years down the road, I discovered the Holy Spirit had led me repeatedly to implement exercises in her life that specialist's use as protocols for aiding in healing autism and SIDS! How cool is that? If we ask Him, He truly will teach us ALL things.

One day when she was about seven, I asked the Lord, "Will you heal Brynne completely someday?" His answer was "You don't need to know that. She will reach her destiny. That's all you need to know." God has progressively caused her to go far beyond how tests and doctors predicted she would go. Even her daddy's death had a healing impact on her life. From the day he died she has been able to connect emotionally and cry, whereas before that time she couldn't empathize or cry. She is an amazing young lady, with the kindest heart and ability to connect with people. She continues to amaze me with her perseverance in learning. If you met Brynne today, you probably wouldn't recognize that she has delays in these areas of processing. The Lord so loves to prove Himself to us and work outside the realm of the possible.

Cindy Jacobs once had a prophecy over Brynne that she had a Chanel #5 anointing on her life and that she would make money. I would remember the word when she was little and just kind of laugh as math and money are her weakest areas of learning. Guess what we found out now that she is older? She can sell anything to anyone when it comes to door to door sales! So once again, the Lord was teaching me to trust Him, the Creator with His creation. He is always asking us to give thanks to Him in every season, every situation, and watch Him heal and restore and renew. He is God and we are not!

If you are reading this and see patterns in your life of persistent sickness, robbery of your finances, and frequent encounters with death or premature death, then research if your family has a history of Freemasonry. The curses unleashed through this are made with blood covenants and at the higher levels are equal with occult activities. One of the ways the Lord had me to pray over myself and my family regarding these curses was to picture the places that were susceptible to onslaught and declare God's word over those weakened areas. Then we named the curses and broke their power with the blood of the Lamb and stood in repentance for my family's involvement. This brought further freedom. I remember when we finally knew that we had broken through. We sold our van that we had been trying to sell for months. Then we started making progress with our debt and bizarre events in which we lost money were halted! When we ask for keys of wisdom, God always brings the revelation eventually! Take back the legal ground the enemy has to torment or harass your family and stand in identificational repentance for your ancestor's sins. Close the doorways that might allow the enemy into your family's life.

Father, in the name of Jesus I ask that you would bring revelation and keys of understanding for my sister/brother. Open up their eyes to the patterns of generational curses and iniquities they have been blind to. Anoint them to tear down the walls of darkness and close every gateway open to the enemy, through prayer and repentance. Help them effectively close every open door from the generations before them. Restore hope to them in the areas they have been worn down by harassing circumstances. I thank You Father, for restoration, healing, understanding and breakthrough!

CHAPTER 8

The Shattered Soul – Dissociative Identity Disorder

Something was wrong – terribly wrong. I paced back and forth in my living room. Fear was trying to grip my heart, yet at the same time I sensed God trying to touch me. My precious husband, David, had just told me that he didn't remember being intimate the night before. I sat down on our couch with my back to Pike's Peak and began to cry out to God. "Lord, help me. I am so afraid. What's going on?" Then in the silence of the next moment, I heard the Lord almost audibly; "Laurie, what is about to happen is of My hand. Don't be afraid. The root of what David has battled is about to be uncovered. This is the key you have prayed for."

I began to cry. I was so tired of believing for healing, and so afraid to hope that this was the end of it. "But Lord, how long will this take? I cried. He replied, "eighteen months." I breathed in deeply and began to weep again with a mixture of hope and fear of the unknown.

That day, several years after moving to Colorado Springs, was not the beginning of our journey to wholeness. But it was the "beginning of the end" for us in our healing story. It was a story about hidden worlds inside of my precious husband's soul. A world created to protect him from the abuse he suffered as a young boy.

Many of you may have never even heard of DID. Its medical term is Dissociative Identity Disorder, or in the past, Multiple Personality Disorder. I had been exposed to this disorder when we lived in Dallas many years before with a family member of David's. DID is usually seen in highly intelligent, creative individuals who have been severely traumatized by an event or events early in life. More often than not, sexual abuse is part of the trauma. The victim, in order to survive their mental and emotional anguish, "creates" other people or worlds to help them cope with their pain. They compartmentalize their world very well. DID is different from Schizophrenia where there are hallucinations. With DID, the afflicted person has created the various false identities or parts themselves, to protect themselves from the memories of their devastating abuse or trauma. With Schizophrenia, the disease makes reality impossible to apprehend for its victim.

All of us disassociate on a regular basis, just not to the degree that someone with this disorder does. Have you ever been driving with your mind completely somewhere else, and then when you arrived, you had no idea how you got there? This common experience is dissociation in its mildest form. When I shut out the pain of my dad's death and my anger at David over unfaithfulness I was dissociating. I like to describe it this way: the soul becomes fractured or shattered by sin. Subsequent traumas or ongoing painful events in our lives, that are particularly hurtful, can cause the fractures to become more pronounced and we begin separating different parts of our lives. We say to ourselves, "This is who I am in my church life. This is who I am in my social life. This is who I am at my work" etc. Someone with DID goes a step farther with severe dissociation, and creates separate people and worlds internally, to cope with the past events of their lives.

In the period of time I lived in Colorado I was in relationships with six other people diagnosed with DID. Only one of them would have appeared to be on the fringes of "normalcy," whatever that is! (David used to say that normal was a cycle on the washing machine.) The rest of them fit in with other people socially and were not perceived by anyone to be strange in their behavior. Their separations or splits had a subtle presentation. They did not fit the Hollywood stereotype of a multiple personality! Please let me share with you our story.

My introduction into the world of DID, was through a family member that David and I were caring for, who began to exhibit very unusual behavior. She was childlike sometimes. She lied habitually, but always seemed completely unaware of her lies. She used foul language at times and displayed subtle changes in her mannerisms. She would swear we had not told her information that we had. Her handwriting would change sometimes, and her voice's pitch would soften as well. As I began to walking with her to help her break her drug addiction, it became apparent that something other than just lying and drug addiction was going on. The Holy Spirit began teaching me what to do step by step.

I hadn't read books about DID at that time. In fact, I didn't even know what was going on and didn't have a name for the presentation I was witnessing. But I knew that what I was seeing was real and not conjured. I also sensed that instead of it being a "mental illness" as the world and some doctors describe it, I was witnessing a God-given, miraculous coping mechanism for survival. I began to refer to the phenomenon I was seeing as a split, fractured or shattered soul.

"Personalities" started to show up in various situations of life. The Lord would lead me to "witness" to each one that presented themselves, and talk to them about being healed by Jesus. Sometimes we would pray for deliverance, other times we would pray for healing. Sometimes the "parts" would simply go away after we prayed.

We walked closely with this family member for several years on her journey towards healing. It was not until many months after she had moved away, that I began to read any Christian materials on the phenomenon that I had witnessed and learned that it was called Multiple Personality Disorder.

After moving to Colorado Springs I was exposed to several individuals with personality splits similar to what I described. To some of these people I was just a safe person to talk to, and for some I assisted them in "integrating" their fractured personalities. Integration happens when the personalities blend back into the soul of the person because they are healed.

So that morning in my living room, when the Holy Spirit spoke to me about David, I was not completely unprepared for what lay ahead of us. David had joked for years that he "listened to the voices inside his head." He used to say he had to "think full circle" to process. This was his way of checking in with all the people in his head. He was terrified that he was crazy. I was not.

I was familiar with all the different parts of who he was and what he had survived. I knew Derek, the fun-loving, partying, gay man. I knew Oliver the controller and mean one. I knew his songwriting part and Max his workout guy. I was just terribly afraid of the process it might take for David to attain wholeness. We both had been in denial about his emotional state and especially the possibility of DID. It was not until we were confronted dramatically with the loss of memory of the aforementioned night, (it can be referred to as "lost time") that we began to be honest with one another and face what needed to be faced.

As I shared in the opening paragraph of this chapter, the Lord spoke to me that He was about to uncover the root cause of David's ongoing battle. It was the voice of God that anchored my soul so that I could move forward and not give up. We had prayed so long and so intensely for the key to David's TOTAL healing and freedom, and here was the answer. This key just did not look like the one we had hoped for! The next step we took after being confronted with this new revelation was to find a counselor.

I had been doing an internship of sorts, with a couple of different counselors connected with our church. I had been in a supportive role of prayer as I sat in on a few ministry situations with people who were emotionally wounded. I had learned that David needed to trust implicitly anyone who counseled with him, so I put "the ball in his court" as to who he picked for a counselor. As soon as that decision was made, we began our final journey. Actually, since the sanctification process continues until we die, this was not our "final journey" but, it was the last segment in our journey to healing this area of David's soul.

The next eighteen months were interesting to say the least! We discovered that healing was needed more than deliverance, although anytime a person is involved in perversion of any kind, there are demonic attachments that come. We learned so much during this time of counseling. We saw that, once the injuries to David's soul were healed, then the various personality splits were no longer needed and integration could come. David could let go of the fractured parts of his soul, which he had created in order to survive those painful events, and let God make his soul whole. We observed that when the root issues were dealt with, deliverance came fairly easily. Telling it like this makes the process sound simple, doesn't it? Unfortunately, the layers that we can create in our imaginations are unlimited. The process of unraveling them takes time and can be far from simple.

The human soul is wonderfully capable of compartmentalization. Some personality types do it better than others. They will bury circumstances and "layer up" under self-protection, loss of memory and other coping mechanisms. As I previously mentioned, I did this myself when my Daddy died suddenly. I was unable to process my grief for many years. As an adult, my consistent cycling with depression finally motivated me to probe beneath several layers of denial, find the root cause of unresolved grief, and finally grieve my father's death.

Since uncovering David's DID, my three older children were recognizing there were some unusual things going on with Daddy. In his healing process, David allowed the personalities to surface more separately in order to focus on their individual healing. My children were suddenly witnessing subtle changes in their dad's behavior. They observed him switching parts. They heard him use foul language and getting very angry. Remember I shared about Oliver, "the mean one," earlier?

We gave them enough age-appropriate information that would help them process what they were observing safely, and we gently explained that Daddy had been hurt a long time ago. We also took them to counseling. We didn't want them living in fear of the unknown turmoil they were sensing. There were confrontations that the kids witnessed between David and me, which if we had not explained to them, would have caused great confusion.

Just once, but once was enough, David's angry part was physically aggressive with Brynne. He slammed her up against the fridge in frustration. I had to face what any woman faces when their husband is abusive to their children. Would I uncover my husband and call the police? Would I leave to protect my children? I spent an agonizing night deciding that I would leave if necessary and would call for intervention if needed. Thank God, that after talking with our counselor, David was never physically violent again! We talked to our kids and prayed with them about what they had witnessed, and David asked for forgiveness from them. They responded as you would expect them to – with forgiveness.

A few years ago I asked my son if he remembered the event. He did remember it vaguely, but the memory was not associated with fear or pain. Children are amazingly adaptable when you provide them with just enough information and make them feel safe. The Holy Spirit was most gracious in helping them easily adjust. Our openness and honesty with our children has since brought them to a trust and maturity in the Lord at an early age. They learned that we all are broken and in need of ongoing healing from the Lord —especially those wounded by sexual trauma. (For those of you struggling to wrap your mind around this part of our story, I would suggest watching the movie, "A Beautiful Mind." It is about Schizophrenia rather than DID, but creates an incredibly vivid, somewhat parallel picture of what the mind can create.)

God was true to His word to me, and David achieved complete integration within eighteen months of his diagnosis. I had really heard the voice of God and the healing He had promised did occur! I am so thankful for the Lord's preparing me through my life in the arena of DID. I am also eternally grateful for our pastors and the friends who accepted us and coped very well with us, through our healing process to wholeness! Without their support, we couldn't have achieved healing so quickly. If you are interested in more materials on DID I suggest reading books by James Friesen, Ed Murphy and others. (See Resource Section) They have written some very insightful materials on the subject with prescriptions for healing.

I think it's important to mention here, that although the Holy Spirit met us profoundly during this season of our lives, David and I both ended up needing medication, to walk through the emotional valley we were in. He had been on medication off and on for years to combat severe depression and insomnia. I had gone on and off anti-depressants after our confession in Dallas. In this season I needed help again. I was crying A LOT and not sleeping. I became overwhelmed very easily as well. I know the mindset that the church can communicate to its sheep that medication is not godly, that it's giving into a weakness. But I know beyond a shadow of a doubt that neither David nor I would have survived these highly emotional seasons of our lives, without the help of medication. If we had chosen to do it med-free, we would certainly not have been able to cope in parenting our kids as well as we did!

If you have been pummeled by life's circumstances and you cannot seem to shake the lethargy or sadness resulting from them...talk to a professional! Don't be afraid of medication. If you were a heart patient, would you forsake your medicine?? The correct medication can help you deal with your pain and move out of it instead of being swallowed up by it.

In crises of all sorts, the Lord is always using the circumstance to forge strength and wisdom in us, as well as healing. I'd like to close with the words to a song my son, Collin wrote, that so describes all of our lives, particularly those who have been shattered by abuse and dissociation.

"Rescue Me"

All that's lost can't be undone
Lay it all before the Son
Holding on to things long gone
Just gives power to those bonds
All that's lost can't be undone

All I want is to be free
But I'm sinking in too deep
Concealing hurt born from despair
Shatters hope of getting there
All I want is to be free

Rescue me from myself
Take control and make me whole
Rescue me from the madness I've created
God I need Your touch, come and rescue me.

You pick me up and make me whole
Once shattered pieces of my soul
I can't rely on my own strength
'Cause in the end it causes more pain
Pick me up and make me whole
Come and make me whole

Rescue me from myself
Take control and make me whole
Rescue me from the madness I've created
God I need Your touch, come and rescue me.

CHAPTER 9

Postures for Healing and Wholeness

So how did we do it? How did we achieve a happy marriage and restoration after devastation? How did we get through the healing process and end up closer than ever, still loving and respecting each other immensely through most of the journey. I can only say that we chose on a daily, sometimes hourly basis, to lay our wounds and negative emotions down at the foot of the cross. We chose to submit ourselves first to Jesus, and then each other. So what does that mean exactly? I'm glad you asked! To be healed is a choice. Trust is a choice. When Jesus died on the cross he chose to trust His Father and lay his life down. He gave up his right to rescue Himself. We must do the same. We must give up our rights — the "right" to be angry, the "right" to hold on to grudges and hurts, the "right" to point out our child's or spouses failures, the "right" to leave. For the sake of healing yourself and your family, you must take your emotions and pain, share them honestly with the Father, and then you leave them with Him.

I can't tell you how many times I had to crawl back to the cross and put down what I had just picked up again! Romans 12:1 says we must choose to lay ourselves on the altar. I chose to trust David over and over again until he earned my trust back. Hear me now — *UNTIL HE EARNED* my trust back! I am not advising anyone to blindly and foolishly trust with no evident reason for that trust. Learning where and when trust can be extended is a process that takes time, time for the fallen one to demonstrate their sincerity and accountability, and time for the wounded one to heal.

I have also seen a temporary separation prove to be productive, especially when there has been physical or severe emotional/verbal abuse or repeated moral failure. Many times the offending spouse's unacceptable behavior does not immediately change to-match up with his/her stated heart change. In these cases, where multiple injuries and betrayals have occurred, there needs to be distance and time put between the spouses, in order to heal. I see it like the difference between needing to be in the hospital to heal from more severe injuries, versus being fine to recuperate at home. A decision to separate should always be made in prayerful consultation with the leadership of your church. Their support and counsel, along with accountability, is essential for healing and restoration to take place. Everyone involved — the couple, the leadership of the church, the counselor — must purpose together to build a new foundation for the marriage and move purposefully towards restoration.

We approached our healing from every aspect possible; the realm of our minds, our wills, and our emotions. We included both the spiritual and the physical realms. We addressed curses, the demonic realm, and our false belief systems, until we knew there were no more big surprises or doorways where the enemy could come in. We approached our healing physically by taking care of our temple. We began eating healthy foods acquiring good habits that would help us heal —I'm talking diet and exercise! I am convinced that we were able to make it through parts of our journey because we took care of our bodies – the temple of the Holy Spirit. Good health habits kept us stable hormonally and chemically — along with Prozac! Watching our sugar intake protected us from escalating our mood swings. Taking care of ourselves physically helped us emotionally by relieving stress and kept us from completely falling apart.

Our understanding and belief in the concept of covenant in marriage, was another strong reason we survived. There was a long season when I had no feelings of love for David whatsoever. That season lasted almost three years. But I believed in the covenant of marriage — if there was any possible way for us to "work it out", then I would stay. The concept of covenant is a reflection of Who God is, and I did not want to betray that belief by leaving.

But I also know that it takes two individuals who are each willing to sacrifice, each willing to be painfully accountable and vulnerable to one another and each willing to die to themselves, in order for healing to come. We would never have made it had David not been so honest and willing to go the extra mile by communicating with me and others. He chose strong accountability to me and other friends. He too, chose to fight for me and for our children by staying, and not leaving. I, in turn, chose to stay and wait it out, to wait until God put the life back in the stretched out rubber band that I had become. I was lifeless, with no ability to bounce back anymore. I felt dead to David, but love is a choice and God is our healer. As I chose daily to give my heart to Jesus, focusing on me and Him, instead of David, little by little, He brought my heart back to life.

Today's world does not teach us to live by covenant, but by our feelings. We see this perspective even in the church as we look at the divorce rate of Christians. We Christians need to do a better job of teaching about covenant. We are much too easily swayed by our feelings in relationships. We often fail to apply the concept of dying to oneself in marriage. We forget that Jesus is always concerned with ME and my heart, and fall too quickly into blaming one another.

One of the names of God is Jehovah-Jireh. It means, very loosely, "God will provide". We're often taught that this provision is financial in nature. However, if you look in the Bible in the first place God uses this name, it means literally, "in the mountain of the Lord, what God requires He will provide." In this passage God is telling the story of Abraham and his only son, Isaac. When Abraham had gone to sacrifice Isaac to the Lord at God's directive, God provided the ram. With this picture we see that the very thing that God required, He provided. So it is with the requirements the Lord makes of us. He demands that we choose love as a way of life, that we obey Him, and that we forgive those who wrong us. He is so faithful and almighty that the very thing He is requiring of us He provides for us.

When it comes to day in and day out living, so often we "don't get it"—this truth about Jehovah Jireh! If God is asking me to stay in my marriage, then He will provide what I need to walk there. If He is asking me to worship Him in the midst of pain, then He will meet me there. David and I both chose to believe that Jesus would help us moment by moment to stay together, no matter how we felt. And guess what? The stirrings of life and passion began again in my heart as we both were healed. It took time. Time, prayers, tears, lots of waiting and crying out to God both together and alone, and God provided His grace for it all.

It also took worship. Worshipping through any darkness is the best remedy I know for healing. The Bible says in Psalm 139 that He is Lord of the darkness. When we exalt the name of the Lord, or proclaim Who He is in our particular situations – power is released! He inhabits our praises. When we focus on Who He is and His greatness, all the "things of earth grow strangely dim, in the light of His glory and grace!" Read the Psalms everyday. When I read the Psalms I would feel encouraged that someone felt the way I did! I was not totally crazy! Cultivating

thankfulness is effective as well. The Bible says in I
Thessalonians, "In everything give thanks for this is
God's will for you in Christ Jesus." It's not that we
have to *feel* grateful for everything, but *in* everything
we can give thanks. When we are grateful to God in
every circumstance, we are acknowledging that God
is the one who knows how it all will end, and He is
King no matter what!

Another weapon we used in our healing was to
speak the truth OUT LOUD to ourselves — often!
The Bible states in Psalm 97:11, "Light is sown like
seed for the righteous and joy and gladness for the
upright in heart." Sow truth, and I don't just mean
scripture — but just plain old truth. For example,
I would say to myself, "Divorce would devastate
my children more than my facing my pain. I would
remind myself and say out loud, "There are few
men who are as good-looking and as sensitive as
my husband. It would be very difficult to start over
with someone else at my age. David loves God. He's
a good provider, etc." When I encouraged myself,
"with words through my mouth", I not only spoke,
but heard, truth.

Speak TRUTH into the difficult situations you
are facing. Use it like a sword to cut through the
junk in our minds and the junk Satan feeds us. God
spoke the worlds into existence. Jesus warred with
the devil in the New Testament with TRUTH spoken
through His mouth. David and I, throughout our
marriage also asked God for the keys to truth that
would unlock our souls from bondage. It says in the
Bible that we have not because we ask not. Dutch

Sheets shares this concept in his book, "Intercessory Prayer", to be specific with our asking and to keep asking. Persevere! We asked for keys to our entire family's healing. Again, God was faithful, and at the appropriate time, He brought the understanding and/or revelation about lies we believed and set us free.

The other posture we had to maintain in order to survive was to stay away from the "why me" question. When I have chosen to trust God and I know that I am His, essentially I have no rights. All that I am and everything I have is surrendered to Him to use as He chooses. Is He who He says He is – faithful, just, gracious, our rock, able to sustain, our healer, able to renew — or is He not?

Sometimes we have to war with our own souls! I had to war with mine over what I felt was my right to leave David. Biblically, I had proof that I could run — he had been unfaithful! But the Lord would always take me to Hosea where I would be reminded that God's heart was always for restoration for His people throughout His Word. Restoration doesn't always happen, but it's His longing.

I had to bring my will into submission to Who Jesus is. Many times all I could do was call out, "Lord help me!" Many of the songs I have written in the last few years are psalms about that season of crying out. When God feels so far away and your soul feels so dead and shattered, He is near. His word says He is near to those of us who are broken hearted and crushed in spirit. Persevere in crying out to Him to meet you in your desperation. Focus on getting through the season you are in – not on how you will make it through your entire life! God has many seasons for us, and they will change, ebb and flow.

Finally, we would never have become whole if it weren't for countless friends and our precious leaders, who listened to us, prayed for us, held us, spoke faith to us and helped fight our battle with us. During that season of the death of my "love" for David I would regularly go for prayer from people I trusted. Corporate prayer is so important. Feeling surrounded and supported by your friends and leaders is so necessary. The scripture says to bear one another's burdens and to weep with those who weep. Accountability is absolutely essential. Without it you will undoubtedly fail. We both were accountable, in each phase we went through, to someone we trusted. Our friends were full of faith praying for us to be free from lies and to be overcome with the truth. They and our leaders battled with us until the revelations of truth took hold of our minds.

The counselors we saw, both individually and together, were a treasure chest of oil to pour on our devastated souls. They confronted us, challenged us, held us, comforted us and helped us see perspectives we couldn't see on our own. We went to several different counselors, on and off, over the course of several years. I have heard countless people say they couldn't afford a professional counselor, but if you want to be healed, you have to make a choice about what is important. We sacrificed in many areas to be able to afford it. We asked for discounts. We prayed for divine connections and for the people God had equipped to help restore us.

In our situation in Dallas, the protocol for our restoration didn't require we seek counsel, but we sought out other pastors and support ministries ourselves. Today there is a whole new crop of ministries available for all kinds of sexual and marital issues. Some have a prayer thrust, some a counseling thrust, and some both. There are places where an individual or couple can go and spend concentrated time soaking in prayer with trained ministers leading them to healing. Many of these places also offer behavior modification that works alongside the healing of memories. Please check the resources section at the end of the book for a list of places I've recommended for you to go for help. I am hearing firsthand, stories of lives filled with tragedy and hopelessness, turning around in months (not years) because of these focused opportunities.

Remember HE is GOD and we are not. Trust Him with your wounds and your future. He is a restorer. For those of you reading this that have already lost your marriages, do not despair. I'll say it again – He is a restorer. He loves to take the shattered pieces of our souls and paint a mosaic of uniqueness and beauty that glorifies Him. But we have to let Him! Your story will be different from mine, but you have the same potential for healing and wholeness.

Father, I ask that you would instill a sense of hope, faith and belief in my sister/brother right now. Deposit in them the knowledge that You are God and they are not! Let peace and relief flood their souls as they rest in that knowledge. Give them what they need to worship and trust You in their situation. Lead them to the protocols for healing that are specific to their situation. I ask that you would grant them divine perspectives about the events of their lives and empower them to leave the past under the blanket of forgiveness. Thank You for being Jehovah-Jireh. In Jesus' name.

CHAPTER 10

Heavenly Perspectives - Hindsight is 20/20

"**M**orris looks at the lower right hand corner of the big picture" was the caption on David's favorite cartoon in the last few years of his life. He had a huge humor file! The cartoon is the picture of a little man in the lower right hand corner of a big picture representing life. Morris, (that's really the guy's name!) is scrutinizing the corner in front of his face. David used this cartoon and phrase as a part of the last message he spoke on December 23, 2001. It really says it all. We are usually only able to see what is right in front of us. We only see the present and the near past. God is, was and is to come. He is eternity past, present and future! He is eternal! We cannot comprehend this with our finite minds. If we can just embrace this truth, trusting in His plan is so much easier. God is working His character in us. Through every difficulty He is acquainting us with Christ's sufferings.

In the book of James he tells us to count it all joy when we encounter various trials and that He will not allow us to walk through anything that we cannot endure. Again, we must remember Romans 8:28, "all things work together for good..." What a miraculous declaration! This verse has been the anchor of my soul since the day I first heard it. I latched onto it in childlike desperation, albeit with a somewhat distorted view of life and death at that time. God has worked this word of truth into me and kept it in front of me my entire life. If we look only at our present circumstance or pain, then we will be swallowed up in despair. Rest in what God has said He will do and hope will be released. Rest in the season you are in, knowing there will be a different one coming around the corner and new grace and revelation will come with it.

When my father dropped dead from a pulmonary embolism, I could not imagine how God could take such pain and loss and turn it for good. In fact, I was so angry at God that I yelled at Him that I hated Him. But in time, God became the One I ran to. He became my Father in such an intimate way. I learned that you can be completely honest with Him about everything. He already knows what we are going to think and say. He has amazed me, time after time, as He has sent people from the Body of Christ to represent Himself to me. I have learned I can trust Him to always bring about His fruit in me and to heal me. This fundamental truth carried me often in my marriage.

When my husband died, I knew some of what not to do from having watched my mom struggle through her despair when my dad died. I knew I couldn't move my kids immediately from where we were living, even though I wanted to run far away. I knew I couldn't go into a relationship with another man immediately and that any monies that were left would go quickly. I knew grief would try and swallow me up or that I would be tempted to go into complete denial. So I took myself and the kids to a counselor. The Lord had taught me so much about the human soul and His teaching prepared me to walk the grief road with wisdom. I also knew from my experience of grief that the season of despair and darkness would eventually end, and the intensity of the ensuing emotions would wane.

Little did I know how many good seeds God had planted in my life as I was growing up, seeds that He planned to use for His glory. I grew up in the theater world and many of my experiences there helped prepare me for ministry to individuals in the homosexual community. When I was still quite young, I learned not only about the existence of homosexuality but I also heard many stories about how sin, rebellion and abuse had led them down that path. Those early experiences were preparation for my marriage and for the ministry God had in His heart. Because of God's preparation, when David's issues presented themselves, I was not uncomfortable or shocked.

Looking back on my childhood, I realize now as an adult, that God had even introduced me to DID when I was just 17 years old. I had a friend in the theater world that had such deep injuries in her soul that one day she transformed into the personality of a very young child before my eyes. I was shocked at the time, but what an incredible "piece of the pie" that experience proved to be for my marriage and what insight for the future counseling David and I did as a couple!

As I shared in the beginning of this book, my large bust made me extremely self-conscious as a teen and caused me to have my own sexual identity issues. But God used even the confusion and internal conflict of that time to increase my compassion for and identification with, those who have been hurt, particularly through sexual sin. Remember David Wilkerson's prophetic word on the "precious seed?" That word helped me deal with those identity issues by enlarging my heart for those wounded by sexual brokenness. God's grace also came to me through my mother planting good seeds in my soul with the phrase "except for the grace of God, there go I."

God allowed all of these experiences in my life as I was growing up, and they were foundational in my approach to life. They created faith in me for healing the wounded soul that He is now using to bless others. God not only healed me but He also is using ALL the difficult seasons of my life to bring glory to His name

In Dallas, during the early years of my marriage, the Lord put on my heart to minister to those who were sexually abused. He just kept bringing wounded people across my path. The Holy Spirit began to hone my listening skills. He would give me wisdom and keys on how to pray for their healing. I would never have been able to minister the way I have, with the same confidence, had it not been for this season. I studied counseling and read everything I could get my hands on about Biblical counseling. I read books by David Seamands, LeAnn Payne, Larry Crabb, Dan Allender and John and Paula Sanford. These were wonderful books on inner healing, and deliverance. I asked questions of those who were ministering in that arena. At one point, I was so involved with ministering to the sexually abused that I considered getting my degree. But as I prayed about it, the Lord said that He was going to train me in a non-traditional way.

I was introduced to DID up close during that time. I encountered several people who seemed to love the Lord and had repented of their sin, yet couldn't leave the destructive cycles of their lives before Christ behind. Deliverance only helped for short periods of time. Working with some of those individuals taught me invaluable lessons for the future with David. In fact, I cannot imagine being able to survive my journey with David as well as I did, had it not been for that season.

Our call as worship leaders was also foundational in my approach to healing. As I walked through the grief process after David's death, it was an automatic response for me to worship at times. For years we had taught and based our lives on living a lifestyle of worship and on giving thanks to God in everything, because He is God and King! That word was alive in me. I had watched God bring good through submitting my pain to Him over and over in the past. Today I can say that God has brought intimacy with Himself to me, by drawing me to worship Him in some of life's most difficult circumstances. I don't believe I would know Him now the way I do without living through those painful events.

Looking back, I now realize that the three years before David's death were such a gift from God to us. We had moved from Colorado Springs to North Carolina to work with a different church, shortly after David's integration process had finished. Our time in the Springs had been so healing and we were ready for a new phase of life and ministry. For the first time in years, I was not counseling much. We fully enjoyed the fruits of wholeness in our marriage and family, during those few years before David died. We traveled and ministered together with our kids a lot during that time. What precious memories for me and my children.

When David was diagnosed with cancer, we needed to raise money for the alternative medical treatment we had chosen. Thousands and thousands of dollars were given to us to cover the costs. The Lord kept saying to me, "For such a time as this." The financial provision that came in was the culmination of years of sowing with monies and time and travel. During our early years of marriage, David and I traveled extensively, especially overseas without ever receiving remuneration. We were receiving from God *years* later. Here again, was the concept of our seeing the "big picture"!

It's been five plus years at this writing, since my dear husband David left the earth. I can hardly believe it. The terrible struggle I had separating my soul from his is a dim memory. The first year when I couldn't sense him and had to break the soul tie that in turn, propelled me towards new life seems so long ago! That year I was so devastated by the loss of everything I had known and loved. I lost my position as a pastor's wife, and my calling appeared to have disappeared as well. Five dear friends died in close proximity to David's death. I lost some very close friends who couldn't go on in relationship with me without David. I was so confused and I thought I would never see or feel true joy again. Then, in the third year, hope returned, and I had the opportunity to jump out of an airplane as a prophetic act of new beginnings. A year before I didn't even want to believe, let alone *actually believe* that my life could be something I could love. The fifth year, my ability to pray in faith for those who were sick, was restored.

I look back at the wisdom God gave me to keep praying that He would keep me safe from my own broken mechanisms and needs where men were concerned. When I finally, went out with a few men, I realized that God had been protecting me from my own fragile mechanisms. I didn't realize how vulnerable I was emotionally and physically after having been alone for so long. Oh that we could see in front of us with the same clarity as looking back! He has faithfully led me through the many seasons of my life.

I loved the life I had with David. He was so charismatic and so gifted and fun. Working together we achieved a marriage founded in Christ and not just on our own needs. Then he died. I didn't want another life! But in the season after his death I was challenged to look at God's word that says the latter will be greater than the former. At first I didn't care if the latter was greater than the former. I liked my life just fine, thank you very much! But as the season progressed and I laid down my own determinations, I finally came to believe that the latter WILL be greater than the former and that it is good!

What is your season and story? Are you willing to let God show you that this season can be fruitful? Are you willing to step out in faith believing that He is leading you into something good?

Prayers that I began praying twenty years ago are now coming to fruition. I started asking God back at Oral Roberts University in 1979 to give me a gift to play the piano by ear and worship God on the keyboard. I had been trained classically in piano for nine years, but the chords and structures of music theory escaped my understanding. I tried for a while to learn, then gave up. What was the point when my husband could play like an angel? But my grief drove me to the piano, and I not only learned to read chords and to play by ear, but I began writing songs that were more than basic children's rhymes! I began to experience God in worship in another arena! I am not getting ready to record a CD of my "Psalms for Grieving." I had no idea when David died that God would be answering those old prayers! What about

you? What do you need to pursue with Him? What
new dream does God have for you? What does He
want to release through you in this season?

Since David's death I have also come into new
places of intercession and intimacy with Jesus that
I don't think I would have achieved had I not been
alone. The intercession for the Body of Christ has
been at a depth I have never before experienced.
Being single and not having to watch out for a partner's needs does have its advantages! I can call up
young adults on a Friday night and they can come
over to hang out and worship. Life is more flexible.
Because of the isolation of my singleness, I have
pushed through to the deepest parts of myself, areas
buried because of pride and busyness. As a result, I
have received much needed healing.

My new healing has, in turn, brought such freedom
from the fear of men and what people think of me. I
am a better example and a better leader without this
fear. God has blessed me with man's seal of approval
through my recent ordination with a network of
churches I have been affiliated with for years. Only
NOW, was I ordained. I am so glad God waited until
I had received a measure of freedom from the *fear*
of man before granting me man's *approval*! What
freedom is God giving you in the season you are in?
What authority has been granted to you because you
have persevered?

In years past when David was alive, we would
say to other couples that we would do it all over again
because of the expressions of God's nature that we
experienced through our pain. We knew we wouldn't

be the same people we had become, without walking down the road that we had traveled. I now say the same thing about life to this point. I would do it all over again to know my Father and my God the way I have been blessed and privileged to experience Him. His love truly is amazing and new each day. He does take our valleys and make them a place of springs.

Full Circle

One commentary of my life I could have made is, "I've had to be a single mom to four kids in their most vulnerable years. I was fatherless. I've had to suffer privately with my own and my husband's shame while the world at large adored him. I've been dealt an unfair hand when it comes to crisis events in my life." And there are many other scenarios.

But God's commentary is, "Laurie, I have allowed you to experience each of these events and seasons of your life so that you would know me in the secret place. I wanted for you to know how to empathize and minister my love to the body in many arenas. I have answered your cry not only to know me, but to be a capable minister of my love and truth with humility." Can you apply this to your own life? What is God's commentary on it? What is His perspective of where you have been walking?

I've had so many experiences in my life that seemed negative at the time, but God is using every experience to bring healing in others lives and open avenues of ministry for me. I've lived through being a home-school mom, a stay at home mom, a working mom, a single parent, and a wife in public ministry. I've been a wife dealing with abuse issues in her home, as well as a wife who is loved and cherished by her husband. I've lived through the betrayals of my friends as well as of my spouse. I've experienced and dealt with depression and mental illness in my home and in my own body. I faced and overcame a spirit of fear manifesting itself in fear of dying, fear of living, fear of just about everything!

In my younger years I was ill a lot and walked through numerous health crises with my family. I know how exhausting and trying to your faith illness can be. I know what it's like to lose a parent suddenly. I've experienced what it's like to become the sole caretaker for my spouse and watch him deteriorate and die. As he was dying, I felt David close me off day by day, distancing his soul from mine.

THE POINT IS: *I've been through what I've been through. You've been through what you have been through. God was faithful to me and He will be faithful to you. He is not a respecter of persons!* In each and every situation we face He wants to show Himself to us and work His character in us. He is always giving us the opportunity to die to our selfish ambitions and needs and see what precious gifts He desires to give us and work through us. He is always pursuing us to trust Him with every single aspect of life. And again I say: He is not a respecter of persons. What He has done for me He will do for you because He loves each and every one of us.

I speak hope and determination to you for your future and for the future of the ones you love! God is not only able to do exceedingly abundantly above all that we ask or think in our lives, but He is waiting eagerly for us to LET Him do exactly that. We are faced with choices every hour of every day that will allow God to have His complete and perfect way in our lives. Will we choose forgiveness? Will we choose the way of love? Will we choose the "low-road" and trust Him to be our vindicator? Will we let Him give us a heavenly perspective on the events in our lives and look behind the curtain of what *appears* to be reality, to see HIS divine purposes that are always unfolding and drawing us to know and trust Him? The truth is that He will meet each and every one of us that call on Him for help.

David said to me before he died that I was a survivor and would make it. I am only a survivor because I am totally consumed with the knowledge that God is God and I am not. I am completely and utterly convinced of His goodness. I am filled with the knowledge that I am complete only in Him. I am choosing to look at who He is and not let the circumstances of my life dictate my response to Him. I have learned in everything by prayer and supplication to give Him thanks in everything, and to watch Him do miraculous things in me and through me.

As I am writing this, I am weeping tears of joy and thanksgiving that the living God called me to love Him, and enabled me to persevere in knowing Him. He is the one that I praise and adore. I am strong because He is strong in me. I don't believe that I would have ever been able to walk where I have walked in forgiveness and healing without His saving power and grace. He made me, and so it was He Who wired me to want to know what made my soul "tick." The precious Holy Spirit teaches us all things and has truly led me from an early age to new life through mercy and truth. Psalm 85:10 says that while righteousness looks down from heaven, mercy and truth meet and kiss. That has been the story of my life and was David's life on earth. David and I would have never survived as individuals or a couple without looking back to move forwards.

I will be eternally grateful for the truths and keys released into the Body of Christ through the various ministries I have mentioned before. Their willingness to dig into the Word of God and bring forth understanding of the human soul and its mechanisms brought the healing we so desperately cried out for. It also gave us the equipping we needed to move out of darkness and brokenness into wholeness and light. Although much healing has been worked in me, I am still a vessel incapable of seeing Him purely or walking sinless – YET. David has attained that perfection and I wait eagerly for the day when I no longer have to strive to know Him and see Him. "But then...I will see clearly." (I Corinthians 13:12.)

I am now back in the city where we lived when David passed, and I am filled with joy at living near my children and grandchildren. I am speaking out hope through our story of victory and watching many come into healing. Every day is filled with joy and wonder at who He is. Will you let Him be all that He desires to you? Will you let Him heal you and use you for His purposes and to heal others?

Let me leave you with these words from one of the last songs that David wrote:

My final resolve is to trust You
To believe all that You do is for my good
And when I don't understand, I will say it again
You are faithful and true to your Word
My trust is in You, Lord
My hope is in believing Your plan for me
My strength is in You Lord
My Life is in Your hands
You're my rock and my shield and my fortress
I depend upon the safety of Your love
And when the enemy comes, into Your name I
  will run
For I'm safe beneath the power of Your blood
You'll never leave me alone
Though the darkness tries to hide Your light
  from me
You'll never forsake Your own
For Your will for me is my destiny
And the purpose I keep seeking
My trust is in You Lord
My hope is in believing Your plan for me
My strength is in You Lord
My life is in Your hands
My life is in Your hand.

Father, in the mighty and compassionate name of Jesus, I ask that you unlock the keys to my sister/ brother's heart by the Holy Spirit. Bring truth where there have been lies in the foundations of their souls.

Send able ministers and friends to stand with them in their difficult places of life, until they receive wholeness. In the name of Jesus, would you heal and restore the wounded parts of their souls. Help them to realize that the posture of trust is the safest and most freeing posture to be in. We choose, in this moment Lord, to give thanks to You the "author and finisher of our faith." Thank you for Your faithfulness to us Almighty God. Amen.

EPILOGUE

A Challenge to the Church

My friend Jill Mitchell and I were ministering recently at a church retreat just outside Austin, Texas. We had shared our testimonies publicly for the first time together. I shared the part of my story regarding David's deliverance and healing from homosexuality and my healing from David's infidelity. Jill shared her testimony about her Christian husband leaving her for a homosexual lifestyle. The Lord had impressed on Jill that we should do a question and answer time at the close of the meeting. There were about 100 women in attendance. We both were shocked when about 80% of the women stayed. This was not "easy" talk – this was straight up! For the next hour plus, the women asked questions and some even shared part of their stories.

At the very end several women came and talked to us both regarding their situations. The numbers were shocking! Approximately ten women came forward to talk to us about homosexuality or bisexuality in their lives. For a few, the struggle was with their father's homosexuality, but the majority of the women had struggled with same-gender issues themselves. The really surprising part to me was that the life-patterns that lead to homosexuality have been fairly predictable in the past. Usually males have had a dominant mother or passive/absent father. They are often artistic and creative and have been molested or introduced to pornography. Females usually have been sexually or physically abused by men or women. This was not the case in several of these women. Two of these women led perfectly normal heterosexual lives until college then they were "seduced" by women and fell headlong into lesbianism for a season.

I had made reference earlier that night during the testimony time, to the "spirit of the age" and that we are now seeing an all-out war concerning sexual seduction and perversion in the earth today. I have been told by high school students in several different parts of the country that the new way "not to have intercourse" is to have anal sex. It was only five to eight years ago that it was oral sex! I have been told that the going "new" thing at parties is to watch girls make out. This same information has been shared with me by Christian kids, not just kids in public schools. In the last few years it has become common to view stars kissing other stars of like gender. Madonna kissed Britney Spears on public television. Widespread acceptance of homosexuality has come to American culture. Are we preparing the Church to handle this dilemma?

Let me interject another conclusion I've come to in regards to homosexuality. David and I researched and studied the "argument of the day," that an individual is homosexual at birth, or is "born that way." The implication of the belief that someone is "born with it," is that God created homosexuality and allowed it to be genetically embedded in the person engaging in this lifestyle. There is no premise for this concept in Scripture. God does not lie and He makes it clear in Romans 1:27 that He is not pleased with homosexuality. "And in the same way also the men abandoned the natural function of the woman and *burned in their desire toward one another, men with men, committing indecent acts and receiving in their own persons the due penalty of their error.*"

As I discussed at length in chapter 7, a person can be born with inherited generational iniquities. Someone in that person's family line opened the door to perversion through their sin, allowing the "DNA" of that perversion to enter and persist in the generations to come. The remedy for this dilemma, repentance, is clearly explained in chapter 7. If the door of the past generation's sin has not been closed then you are in essence, fighting the past as well as the present.

I challenge you, if you are struggling with the belief that you were born with homosexuality, research your family's history. There is a very strong probability that you will find an open door of perversion somewhere in your family's ancestral line. This belief system, if received by anyone struggling with same gender feelings, causes them to quit fighting the good fight of faith. It breeds hopelessness and despair concerning the possibility of living a normal, "acceptable" life, and provides a ready excuse to "give in" to the temptations of homosexuality. We are all tempted by sin. Thousands of men struggle daily against lustful heterosexual feelings. We must fight the fight of faith. God never said the war would be easy. We can't just say that "we can't help ourselves."

I have heard several stories of families with very young boys exhibiting same gender behaviors. They felt helpless to bring healing to their child until they understood the open doorways from the past. As they prayed and repented, closing these gateways, they were able to begin to implement successful behavior modification with their child. The boys began to change their effeminate interests and mannerisms to more male-oriented past-times and behaviors.

We have had our "head in the sand" and adopted a "don't talk about it" attitude for way too long. Fear, not faith, is the basis for this approach. There are not only broken vessels in the Church crying out to be set free from the sin that has entangled them, but countless others outside the Church are longing to be set free. They will not come near the door of salvation until we acknowledges the problem exists and prepare ourselves to minister to these wounded souls. There are countless stories, as well, of men and women who are struggling with homosexual desires but walking pure and alone, silently tormented. We need to make it safe for them to get the help and healing they need. Instead of ostracizing them, we need to minister faith and freedom to those enslaved by homosexuality. We, as the Church, must exchange our judgments for hearts of mercy.

We must rise up and begin to acknowledge that this is a huge issue in the earth today, and we must continue to teach leaders how to minister to these sensitive issues. We must educate the body at large about the ignorant mindsets that have been allowed to flourish. For example, after one recent sex scandal in the Church, I heard of two leaders commenting on the fallen leader's alleged homosexual affair. One of the leaders said, "Oh, he couldn't have done the homosexual thing. He has five kids." This statement reflects such ignorance!

Another frequent misconception I've heard is, "He's effeminate so he must be gay," or, "She has masculine behaviors so she must be a lesbian." These fairly common remarks reflect not only insensitivity but a lack of understanding. I've personally known some incredibly masculine gay men. David, for instance, was not effeminate at all. In today's world, where sports are emphasized, there are plenty of women who dress and act more masculine, who are not lesbians. The truth is that NO ONE, including the homosexual community, fits neatly into a box! Some other fallacies regarding homosexuality are, "Don't let them baby-sit your kids, they might abuse them," and "don't hang out with them, they might come on to you!" I've only listed a few misconceptions being perpetrated in the Church and the world, and, unfortunately, there are many more. We must bring TRUTH to the table. Facts need to be taught. Understanding and revelation need to be imparted to the body of Christ at large. Ignorance breeds fear. Fear causes people to judge and expose without love.

We must also address the mindset that says that deliverance alone is the answer, and healing, instantaneous. My late husband used to quote, "Insanity is doing the same thing over and over expecting different results." How is it that we have done deliverance over and over and haven't gotten the picture that deliverance alone frequently does not bring freedom? These bruised individuals usually need to be healed before they can be delivered effectively. We must face that, for most people seeking sexual freedom and wholeness, a one time prayer event is not the answer. We need teams of trained, mature individuals who will commit to minister to wounded people when they respond to the Spirit's call to holiness and freedom. This requires a time commitment so that loving accountability, patient teaching and listening can be implemented towards these individuals until they are walking in wholeness. Jesus healed and delivered people in his day, and God still performs miracles, but instant deliverance of those in sexual brokenness is not the norm.

We, as the Church, cannot continue to ignore the proverbial "pink elephant" in the middle of the room! It will not just go away, because we ignore it or pretend it doesn't exist! I am concerned that generations to come will fail to hear God's call to holiness if we do not face the dilemma of sexual brokenness and perversion that exists in the church and the world today. We must begin to make a way for hurting individuals to uncover their sin in safety so they can be healed. "By leveling the playing field of sin," we can begin to make it safe to talk about homosexuality and other sexual issues. Communicating in today's vernacular will also help alleviate embarrassment surrounding these sensitive topics. If we are not relevant, how are we going to draw out those who need ministry?

The Church as a whole, in my experience, is not prepared for this ministry. I have watched pastoral teams respond both biblically with restoration, and un-biblically with cruel exposure, to situations of a sexual nature. Whether it is a leader who is in sin or an "average Joe" in the congregation, there is often not a consensus among the leadership about how to handle situations of moral failure. Many churches are not relating to an apostolic hierarchy that could assist and direct them in the process, so the leadership flounders in uncertainty with no obvious place to turn for help.

Even though our pastors at the time of David's public confession loved us and wanted to do the right thing, they didn't know how to practically handle the complete process of restoration. David and I were so grateful that they implemented a plan of restoration for him, even when they were not sure what that process "looked like". They tried their best to minister effectively to us. They did a lot of things right, but that didn't mean they did it perfectly. Most of the mistakes made in the process happened because they didn't have a *specific* game plan prepared for restoring someone to leadership after moral failure. They'd never had to deal with it before!

In our case, we didn't have anyone talking to us about the personal wounds that were being uncovered daily. Our church elders were assigned to oversee our progress and the pastoral staff was basically not involved. David, in his vulnerable state after confessing, was not comfortable spilling his guts, alone, before an elder board every few weeks. Never having walked this road before, the leadership wasn't aware of all the issues surfacing between David and me, and they weren't prepared for the twists and turns that suddenly appeared! Life was moving on for them, and they had to deal with the "fallout" in the church after David's confession of moral failure. It's just a fact that life goes on, even when you are in crisis. A ramification for us personally though, was that we felt outside the flow of regular life and thus, isolated and alone. We had a sense of not being in sync and of trying to catch up with the rest of the world.

One of the biggest catalysts of isolation for me personally, was that I was mainly left to fend for myself as we were restored. I have heard this same comment repeated countless times from injured and abused spouses who have been in this situation. The leadership tends to focus on the individual who sinned. They want to see the sinner restored, and that is a good thing, but restoration of the sinner should not preempt ministry to the injured spouse. When the injured spouse is neglected, or told they can tell no one of what's occurring in their lives, it causes isolation to intensify and the probability for healing the marriage decreases. Somehow, the partner and family members on the perimeters must not be forgotten. As I testified in an earlier chapter, I would not have survived without the support of my friends and without being able to talk to someone through the process.

The ideal support system consists of layers. Friends closest to the wounded (such as friends and family), then the people who help with processing their emotions and hurts (such as elders or counselors), and finally a group of intercessors assigned to cover the entire team with prayer make up a good support team. Assigning teams of cell leaders to minister together with leadership to the hurting individuals is an alternative solution. For example, assign two cell leaders to a couple, or three women to minister to one woman in crisis. They can call daily or weekly to check on issues that have arisen. If you are a church leader, identify other leaders and members of the congregation who can be trusted with sensitive issues. Talk to them about the importance of confidentiality and maturity. Give them training, accountability and responsibility as they step out in faith to minister to broken lives. If you are not able to train them yourself, then find the training from outside your congregation. The list of resources at the end of this book is a good place to start. Equip people in your church whom you trust to be a part of the solution!

I am currently implementing such a program in our church. I am training teams of two or three people to walk a person to wholeness using prayer counseling. Most of the people being seen have sexual issues. Confidentiality is taught and applied. I am utilizing a specific program called Restoring the Foundations to equip these individuals to minister in this way. We cannot continue to live as a Church motivated by appearances only or as a Church with distorted views of what protection is. If you are not a leader but are concerned about this problem, encourage your leaders to get a game plan or offer to help set one up. You will not be sorry.

David and I went back to our leaders several years after our restoration, and shared our perspectives on the process of restoration that they had taken us through. We brought constructive criticism to the table so that if the situation ever arose again, they would have an even *better* game plan. There are many wounded in the Church in need of compassion, wisdom and godly oversight in order for them to heal. If you are a pastor or leader in a church, remember the Bible teaches us that we are to gently restore one who falls. But effective restoration requires that a plan be set in place, especially if we are to get the "gently" part right!

Please don't misunderstand my intensity in this challenge! Please hear my heart – I am not angry with the Church. However, I do feel called to speak strongly and say WAKE UP CHURCH! I love the local church and have been a part of it all my life. I support and submit to my local leaders, and I am accountable to other leaders around the nation. We must change our approach to sexual issues in the Church. If you are in leadership and reading this, please avail yourselves of the ministries and materials that are available. Get a game plan, and learn how to minister practically in the arena of restoration after sin.

Father, if the person reading this has been failed by the Church because of its lack of understanding, I am asking You to bring others alongside of them to help them attain health and wholeness. As they choose to forgive, bring grace and divine help. If a leader is reading this I pray that You would divinely connect them to the source that would most enable them to achieve a workable plan of restoration for their church. Come in Your mercy and power to deliver. I ask Lord, that you would bring revelation to Your children about who we are as the Church, and who You are as our God. Show us how to practically walk this walk of love You have called us to. Amen

GLOSSARY OF TERMS

DID: Dissociative Identity Disorder A mental state, in which, an individual has created false identities in their mind and soul, in order to cope with the pain of abuse or trauma. I refer to it as a "shattered soul."

DISSOCIATE: To function, a person puts aside or buries emotions from the conscious mind. He compartmentalizes and separates events experienced, from the emotions experienced. In extreme cases of dissociation, the person can be unaware they are "switching." See "Lost Time."

SWITCHING or SPLITTING: The changing of "parts" or personalities by an individual with DID.

COMPARTMENTALIZE: To internally separate events from emotions. i.e. social life, work life, religious life. This is a very mild form of dissociation.

PARTS, SPLITS or FRACTURES: Laymen's terms for the false identities or personalities created in DID.

INTEGRATION: The culmination of healing the fractures or false identities in an individual's soul. All the other parts converge into the true identity/personality of the individual. The fractured soul is made whole.

LOST TIME: A period of time not remembered or accounted for by someone with DID. This occurs from unconscious dissociating to an extreme.

UNGODLY BELIEFS: Lies or distortions of reality, that we believe about ourselves, others or God.

GENERATIONAL INIQUITY PATTERNS: Patterns and cycles seen in families for generations. i.e. addictions, pre-mature death, financial loss, sexual abuse, homosexuality

DEMONIZATION: The root word for demonization is likened to us carrying a demon in our pocket. We are oppressed by them but they are *with* us, not possessing us! We possess or carry them.

RESTORATION PROCESS: The process of being restored to a ministry or leadership position after moral failure or behaviors inappropriate for ministry. It requires a time parameter, qualifications for restoration and accountability.

FREEMASONRY: A public, yet secret society in which men and women (Eastern Star) make covenants to support and protect one another in business, and to come to one another's aid. Vows are taken, and curses released if the vows are broken.

RESOURCES:

Elijah House headed by John, Paula and Mark Sanford: www.elijahhouse.org

Theophostic Prayer Ministry by Ed Smith: www.theophositics.com

Books by Dan Allender: www.thepathlesschosen.com

Books by Dr. Larry Crabb: www.lighthousetrailsresearch.com/larrycrabb.htm

CCA/Christian Counseling Association: http://aacc.net/

Restoring the Foundations Ministry headed by Chester and Betsy Kylstra: www.restoringthefoundations.com

Books by Dr. James Friesen for DID –"Uncovering the Mystery of MPD" is one

The book by Tom Hawkins for DID -"Restoring Shattered Lives" and www.cshdd.org Tom offers a weekend conference through Restoration in Christ Ministries to couples with a partner who is DID

Sue Mead for DID and abuse issues <u>www.safehave-nonline.org</u>

Exodus International for same gender issues: <u>www.exodus.to/</u>

James Dobson's Ministry: w<u>ww.focusonthefamily.com</u>

The book by Ron Campbell - "Freedom from Freemasonry"

For Freemasonry Prayer - Jubilee website - <u>www.jubilee.org.nz/</u>

The book by Carol Kranowitz - "The Out of Sync Child" for SIDS issues

For Autism – <u>www.autism-society.org</u> or <u>www.find-inggodinautism.com</u>

For books on worship as a lifestyle and worshipping through pain– <u>www.Hismosaic.com</u> and Bob Sorge at <u>www.oasishouse.net</u>

For CD's that minister to the wounded heart particularly "The Invitation" - <u>www.klausmusic.com</u> and "Pursuing the Presence" a prophetic instrumental – <u>www.Hismosaic.com</u>

CONTACT INFORMATION FOR THE AUTHOR:
<u>www.Hismosaic.com</u>
His Mosaic Ministries, Inc.
5889 Kerr Plc.
Fayetteville, NC 28314

CPSIA information can be obtained at www.ICGtesting.com
Printed in the USA
LVOW11s2303061214

417549LV00001B/2/P

9 781604 776225